Excel 2019
Intermediate

EXCEL ESSENTIALS 2019 BOOK 2

M.L. HUMPHREY

SELECT TITLES BY M.L. HUMPHREY

EXCEL ESSENTIALS 2019

Excel 2019 Beginner

Excel 2019 Intermediate

Excel 2019 Formulas & Functions

WORD ESSENTIALS

Word for Beginners

Intermediate Word

POWERPOINT ESSENTIALS

PowerPoint for Beginners

Intermediate PowerPoint

ACCESS ESSENTIALS

Access for Beginners

Intermediate Access

CONTENTS

CONTENTS (CONT.)

Introduction

This book is the second book in the Excel Essentials 2019 series.

In the first book of the series, *Excel 2019 Beginner*, we covered almost all of what you need to know to work in Excel on a daily basis such as how to open, close, and save files, how to input data, how to format it, some basic ways to manipulate your data such as filtering and sorting, and how to print the results.

(So if you don't know those things, start there first.)

In this book we're going to take the next step and learn very useful ways to work in Excel that you probably won't need on a day-to-day basis but that will come in incredibly handy when you do need them. Things like conditional formatting, PivotTables, and charts as well as a few other little tips and tricks I've learned along the way such as removing duplicate values, converting text to columns, and limiting allowed inputs in cells.

What we will not cover here, because it's covered in the third book in this series, is functions. *Excel 2019 Formulas and Functions* covers more functions than you probably ever wanted to know about. (Approximately a hundred of them.) So if your real interest is in how to use functions in Excel, that's the book you want.

I'd highly recommend mastering the content of *Excel 2019 Beginner* before reading this book or the formulas and functions one (although if you've learned it elsewhere that works, too), but once you're comfortable in Excel *Excel 2019 Intermediate* and *Excel 2019 Formulas and Functions* can be read in any order and are written to be standalone books.

Also, as I did in *Excel 2019 Beginner*, at the end I'll discuss how to find the answer when you want to do something I haven't covered. There are a number of excellent help resources out there that you should be able to use once you have a solid understanding of how Excel works and therefore what's possible.

I should note here as well that even after three books we will not have covered everything you can do in Excel. For example, I'm not going to try to teach you how to use macros because you can really mess things up if you get them wrong and most people will never need them. Also, I'm not going to talk about VBA or how to use Excel to create a database. But I can also tell you that in over twenty-five years of using Excel I've rarely if ever needed any of that.

So the goal of this series is not to cover every single solitary thing you could ever want to know about Excel. It's to give you the information you need to use Excel on a regular basis with as little extraneous information as possible.

Okay?

One other note. While this book contains a large number of screenshots to show you what I'm talking about this is not a book that contains exercises for you to do. This book should be self-contained so that you can read it on your commute or wherever you have time to read it. For me with Excel often the key is simply knowing that something can be done and then playing around to make it happen once that time comes.

Finally, this book is written specifically for users of Excel 2019. If you're using an older version of Excel it is possible that there will be certain things that do not work the same way in your version or that only exist in Excel 2019. Now that we're moving into intermediate-level topics this becomes much more likely.

(I did write a book called *Intermediate Excel* that is still available and was written using Excel 2013. That book was written to be generally applicable to all versions of Excel from Excel 2007 onward and covers most of the same material as this book if that's an issue for you.)

Alright. Let's get started. First we'll do a quick review of basic terminology and then we'll dive into the fun stuff with conditional formatting.

Basic Terminology

Most of the terminology I use is pretty standard but I think I do have a few quirks in how I refer to things, so be sure to do a quick skim of this section just to make sure we're on the same page. This is meant to be a refresher only. These terms were initially taught in *Excel 2019 Beginner*.

Column

Excel uses columns and rows to display information. Columns run across the top of the worksheet and, unless you've done something funky with your settings, are identified using letters of the alphabet.

Row

Rows run down the side of the worksheet and are numbered starting at 1 and up to a very high number. In Excel 2019 that number is 1048576.

Cell

A cell is a combination of a column and row that is identified by the letter of the column it's in and the number of the row it's in. For example, Cell A1 is the cell in the first column and first row of a worksheet.

Click

If I tell you to click on something, that means to use your mouse (or trackpad) to move the cursor on the screen over to a specific location and left-click or right-click on the option. (See the next definition for the difference between left-click and right-click).

If you left-click, this generally selects the item. If you right-click, this generally creates a dropdown list of options to choose from. If I don't tell you which to do, left- or right-click, then left-click.

Left-click/Right-click

If you look at your mouse or your trackpad, you generally have two flat buttons to press. One is on the left side, one is on the right. If I say left-click that means to press down on the button on the left. If I say right-click that means press down on the button on the right. (If you're used to using Word or Excel you may already do this without even thinking about it. If that's the case then think of left-click as what you usually use to select text and right-click as what you use to see a menu of choices.)

Spreadsheet

I'll try to avoid using this term, but if I do use it, I'll mean your entire Excel file. It's a little confusing because it can sometimes also be used to mean a specific worksheet, which is why I'll try to avoid it as much as possible.

Worksheet

This is the term I'll use as much as possible. A worksheet is a combination of rows and columns that you can enter data in. When you open an Excel file, it opens to Sheet1.

Workbook

I don't use this term often, but it may come up. A workbook is an Excel file and can contain multiple worksheets. The default file type for an Excel 2019 workbook is a .xlsx file type.

Formula Bar

This is the long white bar at the top of the screen with the $f\chi$ symbol next to it.

Tab

I refer to the menu choices at the top of the screen (File, Home, Insert, Page Layout, Formulas, Data, Review, View, and Help) as tabs. Note how they look like folder tabs from an old-time filing system when selected? That's why.

Data

I use data and information interchangeably. Whatever information you put into a worksheet is your data or data set.

Select

If I tell you to "select" cells, that means to highlight them. Same with text.

Arrow

If I say that you can "arrow" to something that just means to use the arrow keys to navigate from one cell to another.

Cell Notation

We may end up talking about cell ranges in this book. Excel uses a very specific type of cell notation. We already mentioned that a cell is referenced based upon the letter of its column and the number of its row. So A1 is the cell in Column A and Row 1. (When used as cell notation you don't need to include Cell before the A1.)

To reference a range of cells Excel uses the colon (:) and the comma (,). A colon between cells means "through". So A1:B25 means all of the cells between Cell A1 and Cell B25 which is all of the cells in Columns A and B and Rows 1 through 25. A comma means and. So A1,B25 would be Cells A1 and B25 only.

When in doubt, go into Excel, type = and the cell range, hit enter, and then double-click back into that cell. Excel will highlight all of the cells in the range you entered.

Dialogue Box

I will sometimes refer to dialogue boxes. These are the boxes that occasionally pop up with additional options for you to choose from for a particular task.

Paste Special – Values

Paste Special - Values is a special type of pasting option which I often use to remove formulas from my data or to remove a pivot table but keep the table it created. If I tell you to Paste Special - Values that means use the Values paste option which is the one with a 123 on the clipboard.

Dropdown

I will occasionally refer to a dropdown or dropdown menu. This is generally a list of potential choices that you can select from if you right-click on your worksheet or on one of the arrows next to an option in the tabs at the top. For example, if you go to the Home tab and click on the arrow under Paste, you will see additional options listed in a paste dropdown menu.

Task Pane

I am going to call the separate standalone pane that appears on the right-hand side of the screen on occasion a task pane. These appear for PivotTables, charts, and the Help function.

Conditional Formatting

Alright then. Let's dive right in with a conversation about conditional formatting.

What is it and why would you want to use it?

At its most basic, conditional formatting is a set of rules you can apply to your data that help you see when certain criteria have been met.

I, for example, use it in my budget worksheet where I list my bank account values. I have minimum balance requirements on my checking and savings accounts, so both of the cells where I list those minimum required balances are set up with conditional formatting that will color those cells red if the balance in either account drops below the minimum requirement.

This helps remind me of those requirements, because I'm not always thinking about them when I move money around.

Another example of how to use conditional formatting would be if you track payments people owe you in Excel. You could either set up conditional formatting to flag when a payment is more than 30 days past its due date or when the date is outside of a specified range.

Conditional formatting is also useful when you have a set of data and want to easily flag certain results as good or bad. In my prior career I had to look for customer transactions where the customer paid a commission of over 5%. Sometimes there were thousands of lines of data, but I could have set up a conditional formatting rule that shaded any value over 5% red which would have made it very easy to scan my results and see the ones that were too high.

Even better, you can actually combine conditional formatting with filtering so that you first apply your conditional formatting (in this case turning all values over 5% red) and then your filter the data using Cell Color or Font Color so that you're only seeing the rows with data that was flagged.

The easiest way to see how conditional formatting works is to walk through an example. So let's do that.

Highlight Cells Rules

One of my favorite things to create in Excel is a two-variable analysis grid. This takes one item, say price, and puts it across the top of a table. And then takes another item, say units sold, and puts that down the side of the table. The center of the table is then a calculation of the result for all possible combinations of your two variables.

Here is one I already built that calculates the amount earned at various combinations of price and units sold.

		Price				
		$1	**$2**	**$3**	**$4**	**$5**
	10	$10	$20	$30	$40	$50
Units	**25**	$25	$50	$75	$100	$125
	100	$100	$200	$300	$400	$500
	500	$500	$1,000	$1,500	$2,000	$2,500

See the prices along the top and the units along the side and how at the intersection of each price and unit combination the value is the price multiplied times the number of units?

Now. Let's say that you need to earn at least $500 in order to make a profit on selling whatever this product is. There are a number of ways to do that. You could sell 500 units for $1. You could sell 100 units for $5.

It's possible to just look through the values and manually identify the ones that are over $500, but this is where conditional formatting can be incredibly helpful.

We're now going to apply shading to those calculated values so that we can quickly and easily see each value that is $500 or more.

First step, highlight the cells we want to apply our formatting to.

Next, we go the Styles section of the Home tab and click on the arrow under Conditional Formatting to see the dropdown menu.

We're going to choose the first option in that dropdown which is Highlight Cells Rules. If you hold your mouse over that text it will bring up a secondary dropdown menu with a large variety of choices.

Specifically, you can choose from Greater Than, Less Than, Between, Equal To, Text That Contains, A Date Occurring, and Duplicate Values. There's also a More Rules option at the bottom that will bring up the New Formatting Rule dialogue box. But for now we're going to choose Greater Than.

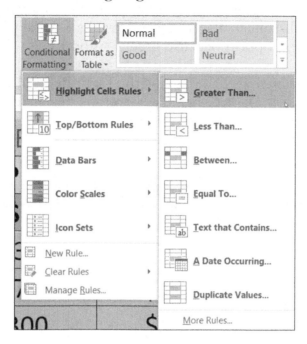

This brings up the Greater Than dialogue box which has two inputs. On the left-hand side you specify the value that you want to use for your greater than condition and on the right-hand side you choose the type of format you want to apply to your cells if that condition is met.

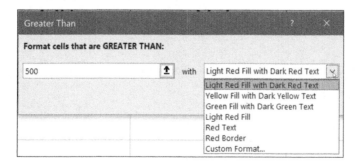

In the screenshot above I have actually made an error in what I chose. Because this is a GREATER THAN condition which means if I enter 500 then only values above 500 will be formatted the way I want. What I need to enter is 499.99 instead.

You can't see it here, but as you enter your values in the dialogue box and choose your formatting Excel will apply that formatting to the worksheet so you can see what the result is going to be before you give the final OK. In a scenario like this one where I want to flag the good results I usually use the Green Fill with Dark Green Text option because green = good, red = bad, at least in the U.S.

For a basic, simple analysis like this one the Light Red Fill with Dark Red Text and the Green Fill with Dark Green Text options usually do all you need. But there is a Custom Format option at the bottom of that dropdown that will let you apply pretty much any formatting you want via the Format Cells dialogue box.

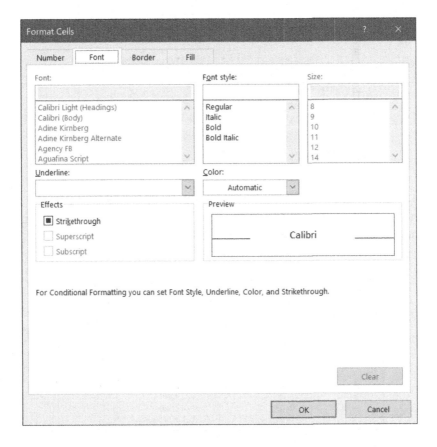

Font and Font Size are grayed out, but borders, fill color, font style, number format, etc. are all available.

I was just able to choose to format my text with a purple font and in italics. But let's just change that back to Green with Green and click OK.

Here we are:

		Price				
		$1	$2	$3	$4	$5
Units	**10**	$10	$20	$30	$40	$50
	25	$25	$50	$75	$100	$125
	100	$100	$200	$300	$400	$500
	500	$500	$1,000	$1,500	$2,000	$2,500

Compare this to our earlier version of the grid and you can see that there are now six cells that have shading on them. (And if this were in color you'd see that they are green with green text.)

All six of those cells meet our condition of being equal to or greater than $499.99. Now,with a simple glance we can see what combinations of price and units get us to our goal.

The other options in that Highlight Cells Rules dropdown work basically the exact same way. Each one you select will bring up a dialogue box where you input your parameter and select your formatting. The only real difference is what type of analysis it's doing. (Greater Than, Less Than, etc.)

The duplicate values option is a little weird because it doesn't discriminate between different values. In our sample data table we have two cells with a value of $50, two cells with a value of $100, and two cells with a value of $500. If I select the cells in my data table and tell Excel to highlight duplicate values, this is what I get:

		Price				
		$1	$2	$3	$4	$5
Units	**10**	$10	$20	$30	$40	$50
	25	$25	$50	$75	$100	$125
	100	$100	$200	$300	$400	$500
	500	$500	$1,000	$1,500	$2,000	$2,500

Even though there are three separate values that are duplicated, all six cells with duplicate values are formatted the exact same way.

I personally don't find that tremendously useful because I then still have to distinguish between the $50, $100, and $500 values. Most times when I'm looking for duplicates it is so I can eliminate one (or more) entry with the same value.

The date option is a bit odd as well because you can't specify a date or date range to use. It only lets you flag a date occurring yesterday, today, tomorrow, in the last seven days, last week, this week, next week, last month, this month, or next month.

Depending on what you want to use it for, those options could be very useful or very limited.

Top/Bottom Rules

The next set of conditional formatting rules you can use are called Top/Bottom Rules.

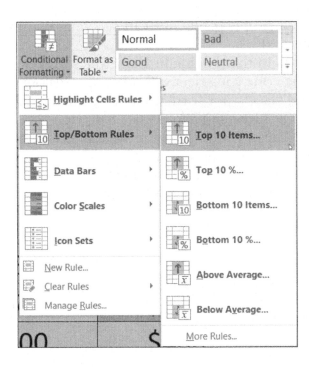

With the Top/Bottom Rules, you can format values that fall in the top X of your range (like top 10), the bottom X of your range, the top X% of your range, the bottom X% of your range, above the average for the range, or below the average for the range.

(While the options are labeled Top 10 Items, Top 10%, etc. when you click on them you'll see that you can adjust the number to whatever you want to use.)

For example, here is the Top 10 items dialogue box.

In the screenshot above you can see that I've changed the value so that it will format the top 16 values instead of the top 10. You can use the arrows there next to the number or click into the box and type in the number you want.

As with the Highlight Cells Rules you have the same set of preset dropdown format options or can choose Custom Format at the bottom of the list.

Data Bars

Data bars are where things start to get interesting. Up until now you could have technically gone through and manually formatted your data to get the same effect as the highlight cells rules or the top/bottom rules.

(It would be a bad idea, because conditional formatting adjusts with your data whereas manually doing that exact same formatting to flag values only works if your data never changes again. But technically they'd *look* the same in that moment in time.)

Data bars, however, place a bar in each cell where the length of the bar is determined by how big the value in that cell is compared to all other values in the selected range.

Your options in the secondary dropdown menu are mostly just formatting-related options. You can choose different default colors, namely blue, green, red, orange, light blue, and purple. And you can choose between a solid bar and a gradient bar.

The easiest way to see the difference between the solid and the gradient option is to look at it. So let's do that. In the screenshot below the gradient option is on the left-hand side and the solid option is on the right-hand side. Both of these were done in the "light blue" color.

Gradient Bar	Solid Bar
1	1
2	2
3	3
4	4
5	5
6	6
7	7
8	8
9	9
10	10

With data bars you can change the settings so that only the bar shows and the number is hidden, but we'll talk about that in a moment after we talk about Color Scales and Icon Sets.

Color Scales

Color Scales is one I actually use quite often. I have an Excel spreadsheet that shows the amount of revenue I've earned each month as well as the amount I've spent on ads each month and for each of those columns I have color scales applied that quickly show me the months where I either earned the most or spent the most.

So what do color scales do? They color a cell a shade of color along a spectrum based upon the relative value in that cell compared to the rest of the range.

Just like with data bars, the secondary dropdown menu on this one is basically preset color choices. You have red/yellow/green, red/white/green, red/white/blue, shades of red, shades of green, and green/yellow and you can choose those to go in either direction.

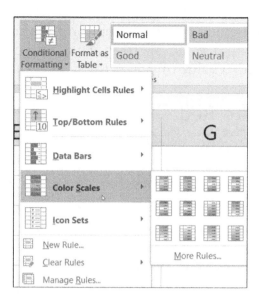

What I mean by that is that you can, for example with the red/yellow/green option shade the smallest values red and the largest values green or you can shade the smallest values green and the largest values red. It all depends on what is "good" or "bad" in your particular scenario.

I will add a comment here to be careful about color-coding when your color choices are arbitrary. For example, that red/white/blue option is meaningless to me. Red and green are commonly used together to represent "bad" and "good" results but when you replace green with blue my mind does not automatically assume that blue is bad so then I'm left looking at shaded cells and wondering what to make of it.

In another scenario I saw recently someone had used shading that was applied to values ranging from -100 to 100. Zero was neutral, -100 was good, 100 was bad. But they had used just one color so it was all shades of red which made the zero results, which were neutral, look like they were bad results. In that example, the green/yellow/red scale or something like it would've been a better choice.

We'll get into customization in a moment, but this is one where I like to choose a custom color to use for my scales just because I find the default choices of red and green boring.

Another thing to keep in mind with this one is that you may have to change your font color for the larger values because black text does not always show well with the darker cell shading.

Real quick, here is an example of the difference between the white-red color scale option and the red-white color scale option. As you can see, the white-red option made the cell with a value of 10 in it the white cell and the red-white option made the cell with a value of 1 in it the white cell.

White-Red	Red-White
1	1
2	2
3	3
4	4
5	5
6	6
7	7
8	8
9	9
10	10

Icon Sets

Your last option is Icon Sets which are an interesting one because they insert a symbol into each cell based on its relative value within the range. You can see your icon choices in the secondary menu after you select Icon Sets.

There are a number of icon sets to choose from that will group your data into three-part, four-part, or five-part categories and will use various shapes such as arrows, circles, etc. to do so.

In the following screenshot I've used four of the options to show you how they differ based upon shape and number of levels. I've labeled each column according to the description that Excel uses. (You can see the name Excel has assigned to each icon set by holding your mouse over it in the secondary dropdown menu.)

Five Quarters		4 Ratings		3 Triangles		3 Symbols Circled	
○	1	▪	1	▼	1	⊗	1
○	2	▪	2	▼	2	⊗	2
◔	3	▪	3	▼	3	⊗	3
◔	4	▪	4	▬	4	!	4
◐	5	▪	5	▬	5	!	5
◐	6	▪	6	▬	6	!	6
◕	7	▪	7	▬	7	!	7
◕	8	▪	8	▲	8	✓	8
●	9	▪	9	▲	9	✓	9
●	10	▪	10	▲	10	✓	10

So a wide variety of choices.

In Excel 2019 if you use icon sets on your data you can then filter your data by each icon. It's under the Filter By Color option. Pull up the secondary menu there and you'll see your icons listed as filter choices under the heading Filter by Cell Icon.

Customization

What we just walked through are the defaults. But you can customize your data ranges and your formats much more than that.

If you want to use Data Bars, Color Scales, or Icon Sets but you want to set absolute limits for when a format is applied (as opposed to letting Excel look at the data and divide it evenly), you can do so by applying default rules and then choosing Manage Rules from the Conditional Formatting dropdown in the Styles section of the Home tab. This will bring up the Conditional Formatting Rules Manager.

The dialogue box will default to Current Selection and only show you the rules that exist for that cell or range of cells, but you can change the dropdown to This Worksheet to see all of the rules that exist in your worksheet.

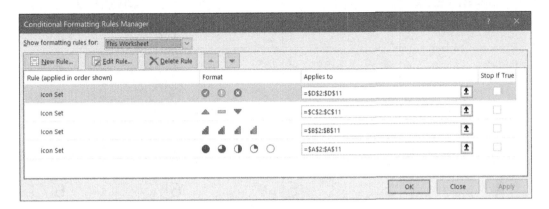

In the screenshot above I have four sets of conditional formatting rules in this worksheet, each applied to a different range of cells.

Note that you can apply more than one conditional formatting rule to a specific cell. When you do that, you can tell Excel by checking the checkboxes on the right-hand side to stop if one of the rules is true and then not apply the rest of the rules.

You can also change the order of your rules using those arrows in the section directly above the rule listing. Just click on the rule you want to move first.

In the past I've had conditional formatting rules where I wanted different formatting on different value ranges and so I had a rule that was >100, say, and then a rule that was >50, etc. Because of how they were written, with that > operator and the overlap in potential results where a value of 150 would be both >100 and >50, the order of the rules mattered.

In this scenario that we're looking at here, it doesn't. There's no overlap across the cell ranges.

So back to customization.

Choose the rule you want to customize, click on its row, and then choose Edit Rule. That will bring up the Edit Formatting Rule dialogue box which will already be completed with the defaults that Excel chose for you when your initially created the rule.

Let's look at an example.

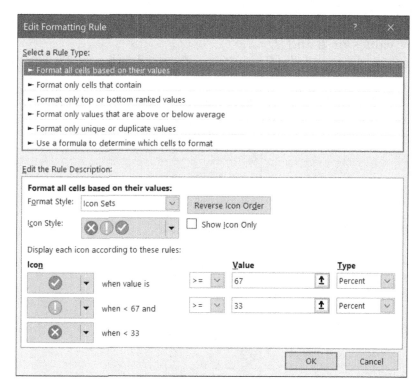

So you can see here that I've chosen an icon set rule that has three categories, the X, the exclamation mark, and the checkmark. Because of that Excel has divided my results on a percent basis where the bottom third of the values are the X, the next third are the exclamation mark, and the final third are the checkmark.

I can change this. So let's say that I want absolute values. Anything 6 and above gets a checkmark, anything under 2 gets an X, and anything in between gets the exclamation mark.

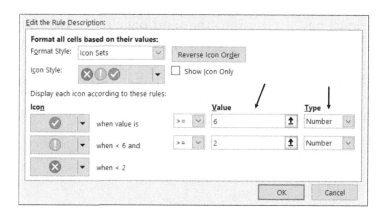

I do that by changing the Type dropdown from Percent to Number and then entering my values of 6 and 2.

Now the criteria are applied on an absolute value basis. This is the result:

3 Symbols Circled	
⊗	1
❶	2
❶	3
❶	4
❶	5
✓	6
✓	7
✓	8
✓	9
✓	10

See the difference? There's now only one X in the whole table because there's only one value below 2 and the 6 and 7 values now have a check next to them instead of an exclamation mark.

Be careful of your edge cases. In this scenario the 6 and the 2.

Because I used >= as my rule for both, that meant that the 2 value was not given an X. If I'd wanted values of 2 or less to be an X, then I would've needed to change that option to > only. (That's the only other choice you have.)

I usually forget to pay attention to that and have to go back and fix it later. If you're like me, be sure to always test those values in your data when you set up your conditional formatting.

In the Edit Formatting Rule dialogue box you can also change the icon set you're using or, actually, change anything about your conditional formatting.

Here's the top portion of that dialogue box:

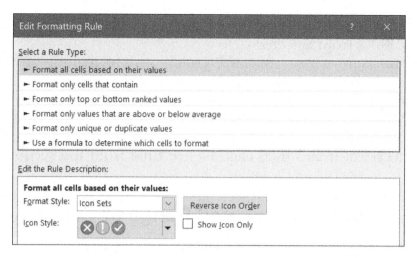

First, see at the bottom where it says Icon Style and there's a dropdown? You can click there and select any of the other icon set options.

To the right of that is a checkbox where you can click to Show Icon Only. This will keep the shapes or the bars or whatever, but it will hide the actual value.

Above that you can reverse the icon order so that the value that was "bad" before is now "good."

And then above that if you read those options in Select Rule Type you'll see that you can change this conditional formatting rule to any of the other options. For example, the third option there, format only top and bottom ranked values is the Top/Bottom Rules.

The dropdowns we walked through before were the shortcuts that Excel has put in place to make it easy to do the most common formatting. But here you have almost complete control.

Remove Conditional Formatting

What do you do if you've added conditional formatting and you want to remove it? You can go back to the Conditional Formatting dropdown and choose Clear Rules from the bottom section. This will show you a secondary dropdown that says Clear Rules from Selected Cells or Clear Rules from Entire Sheet. (There are two other options there about clearing rules from tables or PivotTables that will only be available if that applies in your situation.)

If you've selected the cells with the formatting that you want to remove, just choose Clear Rules from Selected Cells.

If you're not sure where you have conditional formatting and want it all removed from the worksheet you can choose Clear Rules from Entire Sheet.

The other option is to select Manage Rules. This brings up the Conditional Formatting Rule Manager and you can then see all rules that exist for that selection or any worksheet in the entire file. To remove one of those rules, click on the rule to select it and then click Delete Rule from the section above the rules.

Extend a Covered Range of Cells

There are probably other ways to do this, but when I have a range of cells that have conditional formatting on them and I add to the values but my new values are not included in the formatting range, I go to the Manage Rules option to fix this.

It's tempting to think that you can use the Format Painter to do this—just click on one of the cells with your conditional formatting and then click on the new cell range. But the problem with doing so is that Excel treats those new cells as a new range. So the formatting transfers, but the range you had before and the new range are evaluated separately.

For an absolute value scenario like the one we created above, that's not a problem. For a relative value scenario, it is. See here:

	5		5
	6		6
	7		7
	8		8
	9		9
	10		10

What I did for both of these columns is remove the conditional formatting from the cells for 8, 9, and 10 and then reapplied it using Format Painter.

The example on the left is one where the conditional formatting rule is relative. The bottom 1/3 of values get a down arrow, the middle 1/3 get a bar, and the top 1/3 get an up arrow.

You can see here that 8, 9, and 10 were treated as their own group for purposes of assigning an icon which is why the 8 has a down arrow and the 9 has a bar even though they are in a column of numbers ranging from 1 through 10.

The column on the right is the one we edited earlier where we had absolute values in our criteria. Any value 6 or above got a checkmark. Using Format Painter in this scenario worked because the criteria are absolute.

Rather than go through that mental gymnastics, I just always use the Manage Rules option to extend my cell range. Although that can have its issues as well.

To do this, go to the Conditional Formatting dropdown in the Styles section of the Home tab and choose Manage Rules. This will let you see each rule and the cell range it applies to. (In the Applies To column.)

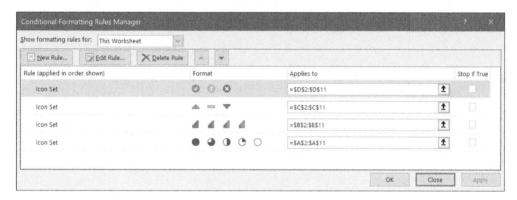

If you're just extending a range, click into that box, backspace to delete the current last row value and type in the new row value and then hit enter. If you want to put a second, non-continuous cell range, you can do so by using a comma and typing in the new range.

This approach works well as long as you don't try using the arrow keys. Click into that box and use the arrow key and Excel tries to be helpful and gives you the next cell in your worksheet from the one you had selected when you opened the dialogue box. It basically erases what was already in there and replaces it with a cell selection you don't want.

(Ctrl + Z , undo, is your friend when things like that happen.)

There is also an arrow with a bar under it at the end of the listed cell range. You can click on that and it will show you in the worksheet which cells the formatting currently applies to. You can then click into your worksheet and highlight the cells you want it to apply to and you'll see a small dialogue box that updates with the new range. Hit enter when you're done with your selection and it will update.

Okay, so that was probably more than you ever wanted to know about conditional formatting. Now on to something much simpler: Inserting Symbols.

Insert Symbols

This doesn't come up often, which is why I included it in this book instead of the beginner book. But I do occasionally want to insert a symbol into a field. For example, maybe I want to use the € sign for Euros or the £ sign for British Pounds. There are shortcuts you can type that will insert them, but I don't do it often enough to know them.

Another time I've used symbols is in my tracking of my short story submissions where I used stars and exes to indicate which stories had received personal rejections from a market and which had received form rejections.

Inserting a symbol is a very straight-forward process. You can either insert a symbol into its own cell or as part of text within a cell. Like this:

	A
1	It cost €25
2	☺

In Cell A1 I typed text and then inserted the Euros symbol. In Cell A2 I just inserted a smiley face symbol.

Once a symbol is there, you can treat it just like text and change the font size or the font color. DO NOT change the font, though. For a lot of these that's what determines the symbol you're seeing. For example, that smiley face symbol is actually what a capital J looks like in the Wingdings font.

So how do you do this? How do you insert a symbol?

Simple.

First, click into the cell or the portion of the cell where you want to add the symbol.

Next, go to the Insert tab and click on Symbol in the Symbols section on the right-hand side. This will bring up the Symbol dialogue box:

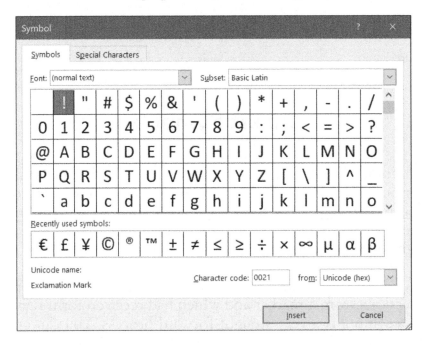

If you've recently used the symbol you're looking for it will be under Recently Used Symbols at the bottom of the dialogue box. By default this section contains some commonly use symbols that you can see above.

Otherwise, you can scroll through the displayed letters and symbols until you find the one you want. That subset dropdown menu will let you narrow the results down if you already have an idea where the symbol you want is located.

Another option is to change the font dropdown to find a font that has a lot of shapes or symbols in it. The most common for that are Wingdings, Wingdings 2, and Wingdings 3.

There is also a Special Characters tab that you can click on at the top where you can find things like the copyright symbol, trademark symbol, and section symbol.

When you find what you're looking for, click on the symbol so that it's highlighted and then click on Insert at the bottom of the dialogue box. In the cell where you inserted the symbol you will now see the symbol.

One more thing to note is that in the Excel worksheet the symbol will appear like what you saw in the Symbol dialogue box, but in the formula bar it will appear as the character it is in that particular font, if applicable.

So here I have the smiley face next to a trademark symbol. You can see that in the cell. In the formula bar above it you can see the capital J for the smiley face and the trademark symbol for the trademark. And above that you can see that this is the Wingdings font being used in this cell.

That's it. It's that simple. Just remember that a lot of the symbols you'll insert are driven by the font choice, so if you do insert symbols into your file be very careful about using the Format Painter or selecting all and changing the font, because you may end up erasing any symbol you inserted and be left with weird letters or other characters in the midst of your text instead.

Hide Rows or Columns

We'll jump into PivotTables in a minute, but first I want to cover another easy little trick you may need, which is how to hide rows or columns. This can come in very useful at times.

For example, I have an advertising tracker that I use where I have to input various values like the title, the advertiser I used, the amount spent, and then the results information. I want all of that information, but it comes from different sources so sometimes I'm inputting information in Columns C and M but not any of the columns in between. Being able to hide those columns so that I can jump straight from Column C to Column M saves me a lot of time and effort.

(I also sometimes use grouping data for this one, we'll cover that one next.)

Another way to use this is if you enter information into a worksheet that you need in that worksheet, say for calculation purposes, but you don't need to see it all the time. You can just hide the rows with that data in them.

Use hide when it's more of a permanent solution, use group when it's temporary or you expect to repeatedly hide and unhide the row or columns. Also, I use hide when I already have group on a set of rows or columns and need to hide a subset of them.

So how do you do this? First, select the column(s) or row(s) you want to hide, right-click and choose Hide from the dropdown menu. Excel will hide that column(s) or row(s) and you will now see that your column lettering or row numbering skips the hidden column(s) or row(s).

In the below screenshot you can see that I've hidden Column B and I've hidden Row 2. If you recall, filtering will do this as well where it skips a row number, but the way to tell which one is in place is to look at the color of the row numbers. With filtering, they are colored blue, with hiding a row, they are not.

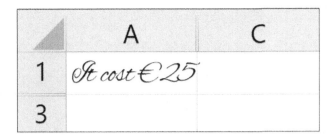

Also, with hiding you'll see that little double line between the row or column identifiers that indicates at least one row or column is hidden. (This will look the same regardless of the number of rows or columns you've hidden.)

To unhide a column(s) or row(s) you've hidden, select the columns or the rows on either side of the hidden column(s) or row(s). So above I'd select Columns A and C or Rows 1 and 3. Right-click and choose Unhide from the dropdown.

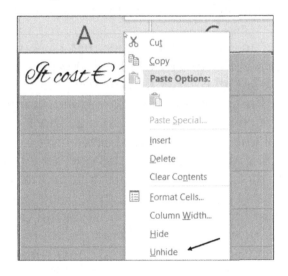

One thing to keep in mind when unhiding column(s) or row(s) is that it will unhide all of the hidden columns or rows between those two columns or those two rows. So if you've hidden Columns B, C, D, and E, for example, when you select Columns A and F and choose Unhide all four columns will be unhidden.

There is no way that I'm aware of to just unhide Column B or Column D and leave the others hidden. Even if each one was hidden individually, they all unhide as a group.

Group Data

There's another way to temporarily hide columns or rows and that's by using the grouping data option.

This allows you to group rows or columns so that you can easily hide them or show them once again by simply clicking on a plus or minus sign.

To do this, select a range of columns or a range of rows that you want to group together.

The columns or rows you group have to be adjacent. If you try to group non-adjacent columns or rows you'll get an error message. (Which is different from how it works with PivotTables.)

Here's my data. In this example I'm going to group address, product, unit, and unit cost so that I only see a customer name and total cost.

	A	B	C	D	E	F
1	Customer	Address	Product	Unit	Unit Cost	Total Cost
2	Jones	123 Sunny Lane	Widgets	10	$2.00	$20.00
3	Smith	456 Dreary Ct	Whatsits	5	$4.00	$20.00
4	Hernandez	321 Spruce St	Widgets	3	$2.00	$6.00

So I select Columns B, C, D, and E. I then go to the Outline section of the Data tab and click on Group.

Above my four columns that I wanted hidden as well as the next column there will now appear a line with a negative sign at the end. The columns are not yet hidden, but they are grouped at this point.

It will look like this:

	A	B	C	D	E	F
1	**Customer**	**Address**	**Product**	**Unit**	**Unit Cost**	**Total Cost**
2	Jones	123 Sunny Lane	Widgets	10	$2.00	$20.00
3	Smith	456 Dreary Ct	Whatsits	5	$4.00	$20.00
4	Hernandez	321 Spruce St	Widgets	3	$2.00	$6.00

If we were grouping rows, the line and the negative sign would appear along the left-hand side of the table.

To hide the columns (or rows if you grouped rows) you simply click on that negative sign. All columns or rows that are covered by the line will be hidden. It looks like this for our example:

	A	F
1	**Customer**	**Total Cost**
2	Jones	$20.00
3	Smith	$20.00
4	Hernandez	$6.00

The minus sign is now a plus sign and if you want to see the hidden columns once more you can simply click on that plus sign.

To ungroup a specific set of columns or rows, highlight them once more and then click on Ungroup from the Outline section of the Data tab.

To remove all grouping from a worksheet use Clear Outline in the dropdown menu under Ungroup in the Outline section of the Data tab.

Subtotal Data

In the same section as Group there is also an option called Subtotal that basically takes grouping your data one level further by also subtotaling it. I've used this in the past with a table that lists month, year, units sold, and amount earned for my books where I then wanted to have the yearly totals and be able to hide the monthly values at will.

Someone could just as easily use subtotals to get summary information by customer or product.

The way subtotal works is that at each change in your specified column value (such as year) it will subtotal the values in another column(s) in your data (such as amount earned).

It is not smart about this, though. If you don't sort your data first, you will have a problem because it will subtotal at each change in your column value meaning you could have multiple subtotals for the same value.

I'll show you an example in a moment, but first let's subtotal some data.

Highlight your selected data and in the Outline section of the Data tab choose Subtotal.

If you selected all cells in your worksheet, by clicking in the corner or using Ctrl + A, you may get a dialogue box that says that Excel can't determine what row to use for data labels. If you want it to use the first row, you can continue by selecting OK.

If you select just your data but not the header row you'll see a different dialogue box that asks if you meant to use the row directly above your data as your header row. Click Yes if that's the case.

Either way you will now see the Subtotal dialogue box where you can tell Excel which column to use for subtotals, which columns to add a subtotal to, and the function that you want Excel to use. (It's called subtotaling and the default is to sum the values, but the dropdown menu actually lets you take not just the sum but the count, average, max, min, or product of the values.)

Okay. So here's the dialogue box.

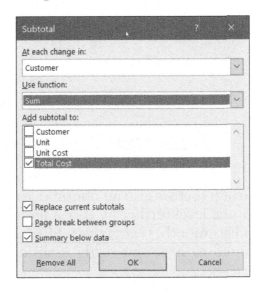

The first choice to make is at each change in what column value do you want to make a calculation. In this case we're going to do Customer.

The next choice is what calculation you want to make. Usually this will stay Sum but as I mentioned above you have some other choices.

The third choice is what to perform that calculation on. In this case I have unit, unit cost, and total cost. It wouldn't make sense to take a sum of unit cost (that would be something you could average though) so I'm going to check Unit and Total Cost.

Below that you have the option to replace current subtotals (usually something you should do), to add a page break between groups (up to you, I'd only do so with data sets where I need to print those results as standalone pages), and to add a summary below your data (as opposed to at the top). The summary will perform whatever calculation you chose on the entire data set.

So let's go ahead and do this with a sum of Unit and Unit Cost for Customer, replacing any current subtotals, and adding a summary below the data.

Here we go. The initial result is fully-expanded, meaning that you can see all of the detailed data as well as the subtotals that have been added in there. But because I intentionally made a mistake here, I'm going to minimize things so that you only see the subtotals.

1 2 3		A	B	C	D
	1	Customer	Unit	Unit Cost	Total Cost
+	3	Jones Total	10		$20.00
+	5	Smith Total	5		$20.00
+	9	Hernandez	33		$96.00
+	12	Jones Total	10		$40.00
+	15	Smith Total	15		$52.00
+	17	Jones Total	2		$4.00
+	19	Smith Total	21		$42.00
+	21	Hernandez	9		$27.00
−	22	Grand Tota	105		$301.00

Can you see what I did wrong?

Scan the list of Customer names for a second. See how there is a Jones subtotal but then four rows down there's another one? And two more rows after that? I didn't sort my data so at every change in the last name, Excel did its calculation. Not it's fault, mine.

So now let me go back, sort my data first and try this again. This is what I get initially.

1 2 3		A	B	C	D
	1	Customer	Unit	Unit Cost	Total Cost
	2	Hernandez	3	$2.00	$6.00
	3	Hernandez	7	$3.00	$21.00
	4	Hernandez	23	$3.00	$69.00
	5	Hernandez	9	$3.00	$27.00
−	6	Hernandez Tota	42		$123.00
	7	Jones	10	$2.00	$20.00
	8	Jones	1	$4.00	$4.00
	9	Jones	9	$4.00	$36.00
	10	Jones	2	$2.00	$4.00
−	11	Jones Total	22		$64.00
	12	Smith	5	$4.00	$20.00
	13	Smith	4	$2.00	$8.00
	14	Smith	11	$4.00	$44.00
	15	Smith	21	$2.00	$42.00
−	16	Smith Total	41		$114.00
−	17	Grand Total	105		$301.00

35

Now I have all of the results for each customer sorted by last name which means I have one subtotal per customer.

Those subtotal lines are each bolded while the detail data is not. At the very bottom, because I chose to place a summary below my data, I also have a Grand Total row that totals all of the individual entries.

I can click on that 2 on the left-hand side to hide all of the detail data and just see the subtotals. That's what I did on the last page where I showed you how I messed up.

When you do that, each subtotal will have a + sign next to it instead of a - sign. You can click on any individual plus sign to expand the details for just that one value. Or you can click on the 3 to expand all of the results at once.

Clicking on the 1 will give you just the Grand Total line.

(Sometimes you have to click on the 1, 2, or 3 a second time to get it to work. I think this likely comes down to what you were doing right before you clicked.)

To remove subtotals, go back to the Subtotal option in the Data tab, click on Subtotal to bring up the Subtotal dialogue box, and then click on Remove All in the bottom left corner.

I've found Ctrl + Z generally does not work well when dealing with subtotals so be careful that what you do is what you want because it won't be easy to fix if you get it wrong.

One more thing. If you want to keep your subtotals, but remove the groupings on the left-hand side, you can either click on Ungroup in the Outline section of the Data tab, which will bring up the Ungroup dialogue box, and then from there choose the rows option which will remove the highest level of grouping. (In this case the grand total grouping.)

Or you can click on the arrow under Ungroup to bring up the dropdown menu and then choose Clear Outline which will remove all levels of grouping but leave your bolded lines with the subtotals and grand total.

You can still choose to Remove All in the Subtotal dialogue box at that point to remove the subtotal lines.

Also, note that which number corresponds to which level of data will change as you ungroup your data but the principle remains the same. Clicking on the number up top collapses that level. Clicking on individual pluses and minuses expands or contracts individual groupings for a level.

Okay. Time to tackle a useful but challenging topic: PivotTables.

PivotTables

Before we get started, for the record I passionately hate how they write PivotTable as one word with capital letters in the middle. But that's how they do it, so that's how we'll try to do it. (I may slip up once or twice, but I'll try to catch myself. While we're on the subject I also passionately hate how their labels and menu options in their dialogue boxes don't use title case and so you'll often see that I do.)

Alright then. Now that that's out of my system.

If you learn one thing from this book let it be PivotTables. I literally chose to write the first two books in the original Excel Essentials series (*Excel for Beginners* and *Intermediate Excel*) in order to teach writers how to use Excel well enough for them to use PivotTables.

That's how useful these things are: I was willing to write thousands of words about the basics of Excel just to get people to the point where we are right now where I could teach them how to use PivotTables.

What They Do

So what are PivotTables? What do they do? Why are they so special?

A PivotTable takes rows and rows of data and lets you create a nice little summary table of that data based upon your chosen parameters.

Let me give you an example of how this can be useful.

Let's say you sell widgets, whatsits, and whatchamacallits. And every time you sell one of those items your distributor (the place you sell through) creates a line of data in an Excel worksheet that has the state where the sale occurred, the retail price, and the net amount due to you for that transaction, and you want to know what you've earned in each state so you can target advertising.

You could filter your data to see this or use subtotals even, but a far better option is to create a PivotTable of your data.

Let's do that. But first we need to cover some basic data principles.

Basic Data Principles

The data you use to build your table needs to be in the right format.

There should be one row at the top of your data table that contains the labels for each column. (I sometimes call this the header row.)

Everything needs to be in that one row. You cannot have multiple rows of column labels. So if you're going to have Year and Month, you can't put Year on Row A and then months on Row B, they need to be combined.

One header row.

Directly below the header row you put your data with one row per entry and nothing else in the midst of that data such as subtotals or grand totals.

Ideally your header row starts in Cell A1 followed by your data starting in Cell B1 and there is nothing else in the worksheet. But you can have data that starts elsewhere as long as once it starts it's header row followed by rows of data and nothing else.

The mistake a lot of people make is that they'll list information in one row and then below that row list a subset of information.

So maybe Row 5 is the customer information and then below that in Rows 6-10 is the transaction information and then Row 11 is a row for total values for that customer.

Don't do that. That is a report. That is something that is meant to be final and no longer subject to analysis. If you're still going to work with your data, leave it as raw and untouched as you can. Once you put in subtotals or break your data up into multiple lines, you can't sort it, filter it, use PivotTables, or create charts from it.

So don't do that. At least not in your source worksheet.

(As discussed more in *Data Principles for Beginners*, you should always have one place where you store your raw data.. You can then use that information to create your summary reports and analysis, or even "fix" the data. But always have that one document that is just the information and that is not changed or touched or messed with in any way so that you can go back to it if you make a mistake.)

(This helps especially if you sort your data wrong because that can pretty much break your data and you can't fix it. Keeping your source data pure lets you go back and start over.)

Also be sure to not have any blank rows or columns in your data set and to have only one type of data (date, currency, text) per column.

Blank rows aren't a deal-breaker, but Excel will treat them as valid sources of data so you'll end up with blank entries in your PivotTables.

Blank columns will generate an error message when you try to create the PivotTable because there is no valid field name for Excel to use for that column(s).

Various types of data in one column makes it almost impossible or at least very challenging to create any sort of analysis based on that data.

Okay. If you want to learn more about setting up your data in the best possibly way, check out *Data Principles for Beginners*, but we're going to move on now and create a PivotTable with one parameter using the following data table that shows state, retail price, and net due.

State	Retail Price	Net Due
AK	1.99	1.39
AK	2.49	1.74
AK	1.99	1.39
CA	3.99	2.79
CA	2.49	1.74
CA	2.49	1.74
CA	2.49	1.74
WA	1.99	1.39
WA	3.99	2.79
WA	2.49	1.74
WA	3.99	2.79

Building a Pivot Table

The PivotTable we want to build is going to calculate Net Due for each possible state. The initial steps for building a PivotTable are the same no matter how complex you're going to make that table.

First, highlight your data.

If it's the entire worksheet, you can just Select All by clicking in the top left corner or using Ctrl + A. If the data starts lower down in the worksheet or you just want to use a subset of your data then highlight the rows you want.

Be sure to highlight the header row as well as the data rows. This does not work if you do not have a header row. Furthermore, the header row must be next to the rows of data that you want to analyze.

Once you have your data selected, go to the Insert tab and in the Tables section on the left side choose PivotTable.

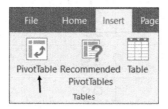

This will bring up the Create PivotTable dialogue box.

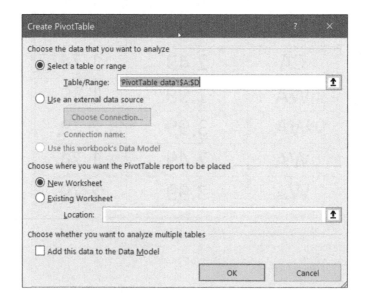

It should already have the data that you want to use selected and shown under Select a Table or Range.

(You could also link to an external data source if the data isn't in the worksheet, but I'm very hesitant to ever do this because if the external data source is moved, renamed, or unavailable that breaks the connection and you're left with a worthless worksheet until you fix that. For example, if you were working remote and couldn't access your servers, no analysis for you.)

The next section in the dialogue box has you choose where you want to put your PivotTable. I always choose to put my PivotTable into a new worksheet. If for some reason you had an existing worksheet where you wanted to put it, you could check that box and select that worksheet instead.

The checkbox for adding data to the Data Model is not something we're going to cover here so you can ignore it for now.

In summary, for a basic PivotTable you can almost always just click OK on this dialogue box without making any changes.

Once you click OK you should now see something like this:

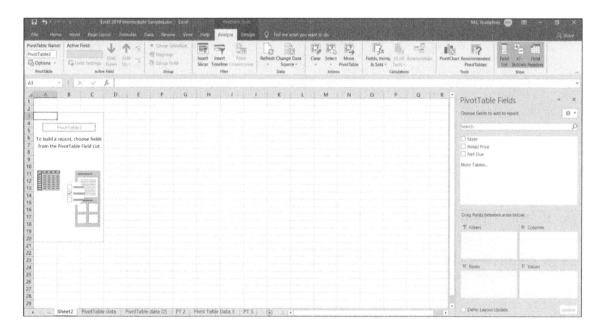

That's hard to see, so let's zoom in on the right-hand side for now.

The top section shows your available columns of data which can be used to specify the parameters used in the top row or the side column of your table, or as part of the calculated values in the center of the table, or as a filter for what subset of results appears in the table.

Our example here is going to be a very simple one that will use just state and then calculate net due for each state. We'll walk through more complex examples later.

The bottom section is where you assign each field to its role. You do this by clicking on the field in the top section and dragging it into position in the bottom section.

So I'm going to drag State into my Columns section and Net Due into my Values section. (You can also right-click on a field at the top and choose from the dropdown menu where you'd like to place that particular field. So I could have right-clicked on State and chosen Add to Column Labels.

Either way, the right-hand side should now look like this:

Up top you can see that the two fields I used have been checked. (That doesn't mean you can't use them again, but it does mean that they are currently in use somewhere in the table.)

Down at the bottom you can see that State is being used in the Columns section and Net Due is in the Values section. You can also see that Net Due is being summed so that the values shown are the sum of the net due of all entries for each specific state.

This is important to check, because often Excel will bring in a supposed numeric value and default to counting it instead of summing it.

So for any field you drag to the Values section, be sure that the correct function is being performed on that data.

We'll discuss later how to change it if the right function is not being performed in the Value Field Settings section. But for now, this is the PivotTable we get:

	A	B	C	D	E	F
1						
2						
3		Column Labels				
4		AK	CA	WA	(blank)	Grand Total
5	Sum of Net Due	4.529	8.022	8.722		21.273

You'll see that Excel places the PivotTable a few rows down in the worksheet. (I think because of allowing room for a filter option up top, but it still doesn't really make sense to me to do so since PivotTables are meant to be dynamic and if I have more than one filter the table has to move down anyway.)

Because we had no Row parameter the table is just two lines. The first is our column labels,which are the various states listed under State in our source data.

The second is the sum of the net due values for each of those states.

That's what it looks like when we build this with State in the Columns section, but since we're dealing with only one parameter, I could have just as easily done so with State in the Rows section.

To move State to the Rows section, you just click and drag it from Columns to Rows. The PivotTable will update automatically. Now we get this:

	A	B
1		
2		
3	Row Labels	Sum of Net Due
4	AK	4.529
5	CA	8.022
6	WA	8.722
7	(blank)	
8	Grand Total	21.273

A table with two columns this time instead of two rows.

The states are now listed down the left-hand side and the sum of the net due for each of them is listed in the next column. Instead of a grand total on the right-hand side, it's now on the bottom.

Exact same results (AK 4.529, etc.) but just displayed differently.

Personally, for this limited data set I prefer this format to the first one, but if I were to add in product name on the other axis of this table then I would want my products in the rows section and my states back in the columns section.

Part of deciding where to put each field is knowing what your intent is when you build your PivotTable.

OK. So that was how to build a basic PivotTable. Select your data, insert PivotTable, drag and drop your fields where you want them, and you're done.

We'll cover more complex examples in a minute, but first let's talk about how to better format your results using the Value Field Settings option.

Value Field Settings

Look at the numbers displayed in the PivotTables we generated previously. In both tables you can see that the values are 4.529. 8.022, 8.722, and 21.273. We know that these are currency values we're looking at, but Excel doesn't know that so it just treated them like normal numbers.

To fix this, you could just highlight the visible cells and change the formatting to Currency or Accounting using the options in the Home tab. That will work. But PivotTables are dynamic and there's no guarantee that if you updated your data and then updated your table that the formatting would hold for the new data. It would depend on how exactly you had applied the formatting.

Change Formatting

There's a better way to change the formatting for the field you use in the Values section, and that is through the Value Field Settings.

To use this option, go to the Values section in the PivotTable Fields task pane, click on a field there (in this case Sum of Net Due) that you want to edit, and choose Value Field Settings from the dropdown menu.

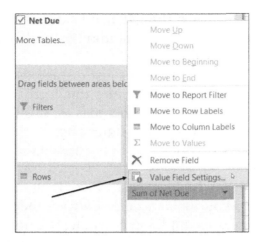

This brings up the Value Field Settings dialogue box where you can perform a number of different tasks, including changing the format of the calculated values in your PivotTable.

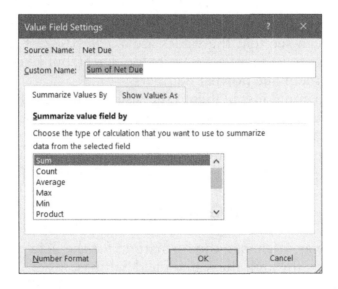

Let's do that now. First, we need to click on Number Format in the bottom left corner of the dialogue box. That will bring up the Number tab of the Format Cells dialogue box that we're all familiar with. (Or should be. It's covered in *Excel 2019 Beginner* if you're not.)

Click on the category of number format you want to use (in this case Currency), and then make any more detailed selection under that category (not applicable in this case). Click OK when you're done.

That will take you back to the Value Field Settings dialogue box where you will need to click OK one more time to close it out as well.

Your new formatting will be applied immediately. Like so:

Row Labels	Sum of Net Due
AK	$4.53
CA	$8.02
WA	$8.72
(blank)	
Grand Total	**$21.27**

Now all of the cells that are calculating the sum of net value have currency formatting and this will hold even if you refresh the data in the PivotTable.

Change Function

In addition to changing the format of the results in the middle of your PivotTables, you can also change the type of calculation Excel is going to perform on those values.

As I mentioned before, sometimes Excel wants to count numeric values instead of sum them. Since I almost always need it to sum, I almost always need to make this adjustment in the Value Field Settings.

To change the function Excel uses on the fields in your Values section, click on the field label that you need to modify, select Value Field Settings to open the Value Field Settings dialogue box, and then select the function you want from the list in the center of the main tab.

You can see (on the opposite page) what function is currently selected and what functions are available for selection.

Sum adds the values together, Count will count how many records meet the conditions, Average will average the values that meet them, Max will return the highest value, Min will return the lowest value, and Product will take the product of all of the values that meet those conditions.

You can scroll down to see more options which include Count Numbers, StdDev, StdDevp, and Var.

Show Values As

Before we move on, I want to point out one other thing you can do in the Value Field Settings dialogue box, and that's the options you have in the Show Values As tab on the main screen.

What we just looked at were the options you have under the Summarize Values By tab, which is the default, but right next to it is the Show Values As tab.

Click on that and you'll see a whole other set of options such as % of Grand Total, % of Column Total, % of Row Total, etc.

If you don't want to see absolute values but instead want to make relative calculations, this is where you can go to do so.

Here is the dialogue box. I've clicked on the dropdown menu that said No Calculation to show the first six options. You can use the scroll bar to see even more.

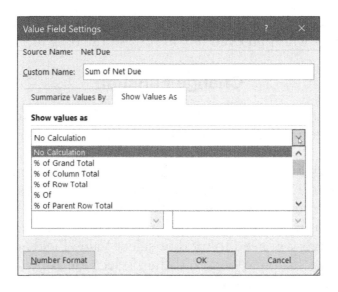

Remember how I said earlier that you can use a field more than once?

This is a perfect example of when you might want to do that. You can, for example, sum a value in one column and then right next to that place a calculation showing the percent of the total represented by that value.

Let's do that here. We'll have the sum of the net due in each state and then we'll put the % of the grand total in the column next to that.

Like so:

Row Labels	Sum of Net Due	Sum of Net Due2
AK	$4.53	21.29%
CA	$8.02	37.71%
WA	$8.72	41.00%
(blank)		0.00%
Grand Total	$21.27	100.00%

Obviously the column names need amended, but we have the actual values in the first column and then the percent of whole those represent in the second column. For example, AK is $4.53 and 21% of the total.

This looks good and is easy to interpret because we're only working with one row or column label. Adding in a column label to that table would start to look messy because you'd have two columns per column label.

So how did I do this? I simply dragged Net Due to the Values section a second time and then used Value Field Settings to change the calculation for that second instance of Net Due to % of Grand Total instead of Sum.

Alright. That's what you can do with the Value Field Settings dialogue box. Now let's talk about some simple edits you can make before moving on to more complex tables.

Refresh Your Data

If you change your original data that Excel is using to create your PivotTable, you can refresh your PivotTable so that it will show the updated results. To do this, right-click on the table and choose Refresh. Or you can click on the table and go to the Data section of the Analyze tab and choose Refresh from there.

Be careful when you refresh a PivotTable because, as I've mentioned before, they are dynamic. What this means is that the number of rows and columns in a PivotTable are not fixed. A PivotTable will shrink or grow to fit the data you give it and the parameters you set.

For example, if I changed the data table used above to include a fourth State value, my PivotTable would expand one row to show that data.

The best practice with PivotTables (in my opinion) is to work with them on a worksheet by themselves.

Do not do calculations or explanations or notes around an active PivotTable. It only takes one slip to erase your notes.

Also, say you wrote a note for AK which is currently on Row 4. But then the PivotTable updates and the AK data is now on Row 6. Your notes will not move with the data so will still be on Row 4 and now look like they apply to whatever state is on Row 4 after the data is refreshed.

This is why I often will generate a PivotTable and then click in the top left corner of my worksheet to Select All and use Paste Special-Values to paste the result back into that worksheet as data. It eliminates the PivotTable, but gives me a data table with the exact same information in it and no danger it will change.

Doing that works for me because I often use PivotTables as a one-off to summarize a large set of data. It would not work for someone who wants to refresh their analysis on a regular basis.

So, again, know why you're building your PivotTable and plan accordingly.

(There's also nothing to keep you from having an active PivotTable in one worksheet and copying and pasting special-values a version of that data to another worksheet. Just be sure if you do that to label either the tab or the first row of the second worksheet with the date you did so.

Changing the Order of Values in Rows or Columns

If you don't like the order that your entries are in, you can right-click on an entry and use the Move option to change the display order. Here I right-clicked on CA in our table:

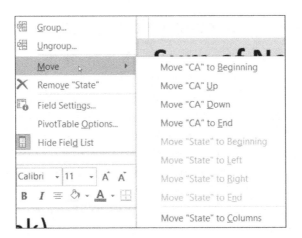

You can see that my options are to move it to the beginning of the list, to move it up, to move it down, or to move it to the end of the list.

(There's also another option at the bottom there that would move State from the Rows section to the Columns section, so that's another way to do that as well.)

If you have a lot of values and want to move them around it's a good idea to be strategic about doing so or else you'll end up moving some fields multiple times.

For example, if I move the field I want at the top to the top first and then have another field I want to move into the second-place position I'll either be stuck moving that second field up row by row (or over column by column because it works the same with columns) or I'll have to move that second row to the top and then move it down one.

I could save myself that effort by moving the second position field first.

By default your values in your row and column headers are going to be A to Z sorted but if you move things around and want to return to that state or want to sort in a different order, you can right-click on a value and choose Sort.

Display a Subset of Results in Your PivotTable

There are a couple of ways to tell Excel that you only want to see a subset of your data.

One is to use the Filters section in PivotTable Fields to place another field that can be used as your filter.

In this example we only have Retail Price left to work with, but that's fine, let's use it to narrow down the results in our PivotTable to just those for products sold with a Retail Price of $3.99.

First step is to add Retail Price to the Filters section of the PivotTable Fields.

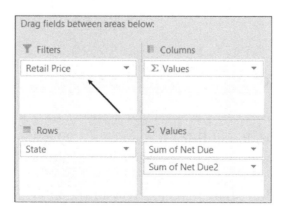

Next step is to go to the Filter dropdown menu that is now above the PivotTable and make our selection from the options there. It works just like normal Filtering in terms of checking/unchecking boxes.

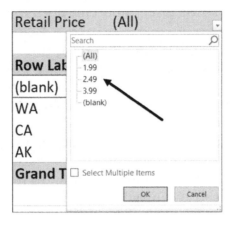

Click OK and the PivotTable will update to only show results that correspond to that filter value. Like so:

	A	B	C
1	Retail Price	3.99	
2			
3	Row Labels	Sum of Net Due	Sum of Net Due2
4	WA	$5.59	66.67%
5	CA	$2.79	33.33%
6	Grand Total	$8.38	100.00%

You can see that next to Retail Price it now says 3.99 which is our filter value. (It would say All if there were no filter in place and Multiple if there was more than one filter choice selected.)

Also, note that we don't have AK as a row in the table anymore because there were no results for a Retail Price of 3.99 and AK. The table updated dynamically to remove that row since it wouldn't have values in it.

That's how you filter a table based on a value that isn't in the table itself.

If you want to display only a subset of the results in your table using the values in the rows or columns of the table itself, you can do that by clicking on the small gray arrow next to Row Label and/or Column Label.

So here we have that option for Row Labels.

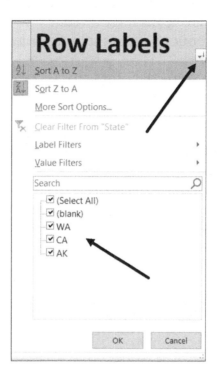

Filtering works just the same here as it would in a normal Excel worksheet. There should be checks in the boxes for the values you still want visible.

You can also filter by a set of parameters using the Label Filters or Value Filters options. If I have a long list of my titles, for example, I might filter by a word that's common to the titles I want to review like "Excel".

There's another way to hide data in a table that applies when you have more then one criteria in your row or column that we'll circle back to later.

Remove Subtotals or Grand Totals

For now we can cover how to remove grand totals from your data as well as subtotals (which we haven't yet encountered but will when we add in a second parameter field to a row or column.)

Click on a PivotTable and at the top of the screen you will see that there is a PivotTable Tools section that appears with two tabs that aren't normally there, Analyze and Design. (They appear after the Help tab.)

To remove (or edit) Grand Totals or Subtotals, go to the Design tab.

On the far left side in the Layout section you'll see dropdowns labeled Subtotals and Grand Totals. This is where you can remove subtotals or grand totals from your table or add them if they've been removed.

You can also change the options so that subtotals or grand totals only appear for columns or for rows.

I use this because I have some data that crosses years, so it covers 2015, 2016, etc. By default Excel adds subtotals to that data at every change in year. So I'll have twelve columns of monthly results and then a 2015 subtotal column, and then twelve more columns and then a 2016 subtotal, etc.

I often want to use that data with charts, so don't want my data broken up that way. I choose Do Not Show Subtotals from the dropdown to remove them.

Same goes for Grand Totals.

As another example, one set of data I work with also involves multiple currencies. It doesn't make sense to have a grand total of currency values when that means you're adding USD to AUD to GBP.

I alluded to it above, but removing grand totals works just the same. Click on the PivotTable, go to the Design tab, click on the arrow under Grand Totals in the Layout section, and choose "Off For Rows and Columns" to remove them completely.

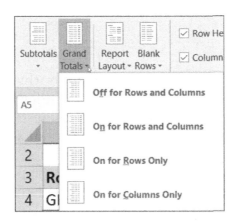

In the table on the next page, I've removed the Grand Total row from the table we've been working with. See how the data just ends and there's no final row anymore that provides the total value for each column? That was the grand total row and it's no longer there.

Row Labels	Sum of Net Due	Sum of Net Due2
(blank)		0.00%
WA	$8.72	41.00%
CA	$8.02	37.71%
AK	$4.53	21.29%

Okay. While we're in the Design tab, let's cover the rest of what's there.

Basic Formatting of a PivotTable

We'll start with PivotTable Styles.

PivotTable Styles

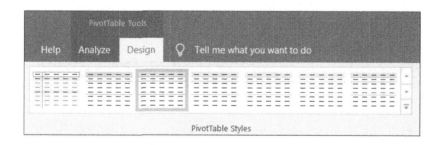

PivotTable Styles are shown on the right-hand side of the Design tab. I can see by default seven different styles. (If your screen is bigger or smaller that number may be different for you.) At the end of the visible styles there are up and down arrows that will let you see more available styles.

A quick count shows what looks like 85 different choices.

The default style that Excel uses in my version has a pale blue header row, no borders within the table, and bolded text for any summary rows.

To change that default is very easy. If you like the look of another option in the PivotTable Styles, just click on it. Holding your mouse over each style will change the table so you can see what that style will look like before actually selecting it. Here are two quick examples:

This first one just uses one color, no fill in any of the header or summary rows, and no bolding in the Grand Total row.

Retail Price	(All)	
Row Labels	Sum of Net Due	Sum of Net Due2
(blank)		0.00%
WA	$8.72	41.00%
CA	$8.02	37.71%
AK	$4.53	21.29%
Grand Total	$21.27	100.00%

This second one uses fill color in all of the cells, a darker fill color for the grand total and header rows, and white text in those rows.

Retail Price	(All)	
Row Labels	Sum of Net Due	Sum of Net Due2
(blank)		0.00%
WA	$8.72	41.00%
CA	$8.02	37.71%
AK	$4.53	21.29%
Grand Total	$21.27	100.00%

As you can see, a lot of variety to choose from and already pre-formatted to allow you to change your format within seconds.

It's also possible to use one of those PivotTable Styles and then further customize it using the formatting options in the Home tab, the mini formatting menu, or the Format Cells dialogue box.

PivotTable Style Options

To the left of the PivotTable Styles is a group of four checkboxes that are located in the PivotTable Style Options section.

You can click onto the Row Headers and Column Headers options to remove or add fill from the row and column headers. So in the last example if I click on Column Headers that will remove the black band from the row that contains the text "Row Labels", "Sum of Net Due", and "Sum of Net Due 2".

With a PivotTable that is using the default format, Banded Rows and Banded Columns will apply gray shading on every other row or column, depending on the choice you make. This can be very useful to have on large data tables where it's difficult to distinguish between one row or column of data and the next.

Report Layout

Report Layout comes into play when you have a PivotTable that has multiple variables in the Rows section. It allows you to choose how your data will display within the table. We'll build this particular table later, but just to show you the different options, this is a table that has both Author Name and Title in the Rows section and is arranged so that data shows for each Author with details listed for each Title.

This is the rows layout when Show in Compact Form is selected:

Row Labels ▾	January
⊟ Author A	$67.46
Title A	$67.46
⊟ Author B	
Title B	
⊟ Author C	$148.27
Title C	$90.47
Title D	$46.50
Title E	$11.30

This is the layout when Show in Outline Form is selected. Note how Title is now in its own column:

Author Nam ⌄	Title ⌄	January
⊟ Author A		$67.46
	Title A	$67.46
⊟ Author B		
	Title B	
⊟ Author C		$148.27
	Title C	$90.47
	Title D	$46.50
	Title E	$11.30

This is Show in Tabular Form. The first value for Title is now sharing a line with the Author Name and the summary for each of the primary variables is listed below all of the entries instead of above on the line with the Author Name.

Author Nam ⌄	Title ⌄	January
⊟ Author A	Title A	$67.46
Author A Total		$67.46
⊟ Author B	Title B	
Author B Total		
⊟ Author C	Title C	$90.47
	Title D	$46.50
	Title E	$11.30
Author C Total		$148.27

These formats are good for a report, but not if you want to perform further data analysis.

For that, choose to Repeat All Item Labels, turn off Subtotals and Grand Totals, and use the Tabular Form to get something like this:

Author Nam ⌄	Title ⌄	January
⊟ Author A	Title A	$67.46
⊟ Author B	Title B	
⊟ Author C	Title C	$90.47
Author C	Title D	$46.50
Author C	Title E	$11.30

See how each individual row still lists the value for both Author and Name? That's what you need if you're going to take this table and use it as a data set elsewhere. (By copying and pasting with special values.)

Okay, then. Moving on.

Blank Rows

The final item in that Design tab that we haven't discussed yet is Blank Rows. With that dropdown you can either have Excel insert blank rows between each of your items or you can have it remove blank rows that have been inserted. This only works if you have more then one variable in the Rows section like in the table we were just looking at that has both Author and Title.

Changing Field Names

One other quick formatting option to cover and that's how you change a field name. I, for example, would not want to have a table where the second column was "Sum of Net Due 2". To change a column name, click into that cell and then type your new name into the formula bar and hit enter.

You can also double-click on the cell to open the Value Field Settings dialogue box and in the field called Custom Name you can type in the name you want to use.

(Or, if you were smarter than me, you would have done that already at the time you were creating that calculation, but I tend not to notice these things until I'm tidying up.)

PivotTable With One Row and One Column

Now let's move on to a more complex example where we have values across both the top of the table and along the side, and the calculations in the table are for when both values apply.

I'm going to add Product and Date of Sale columns to our data. This will give us a second category to work with as well as another filtering option should we need it.

Here's the new data:

	A	B	C	D	E
1	Date of Sale	Product	State	Retail Price	Net Due
2	1/3/2020	Item A	AK	1.99	1.39
3	3/1/2020	Item B	AK	2.49	1.74
4	4/15/2020	Item B	AK	1.99	1.39
5	6/4/2020	Item A	CA	3.99	2.79
6	4/7/2020	Item A	CA	2.49	1.74
7	9/10/2020	Item C	CA	2.49	1.74
8	11/11/2020	Item C	AZ	2.49	1.74
9	12/3/2020	Item A	WA	1.99	1.39
10	4/9/2020	Item B	WA	3.99	2.79
11	9/3/2020	Item B	WA	2.49	1.74
12	2/2/2020	Item A	WA	3.99	2.79

And here's our new selection options pane with State in the Columns section, Product in the Rows section, Net Due in the Values section, and Date of Sale in the Filter section.

This is what that looks like in the PivotTable itself:

	A	B	C	D	E	F	G
1	Date of Sale	(All)					
2							
3	**Sum of Net Due**	Column Labels					
4	**Row Labels**	AK	AZ	CA	WA	(blank)	Grand Total
5	Item A	1.393		4.536	4.186		10.115
6	Item B	3.136			4.536		7.672
7	Item C		1.743	1.743			3.486
8	(blank)						
9	**Grand Total**	4.529	1.743	6.279	8.722		21.273

The values in the middle of the table are the sum of the Net Due for each combination of State and Product.

So Cell D5 which is 4.536 is the total net due for sales of Item A in CA. (The AK amounts are a little hard to read right now because the width of Column B is based on the text "Column Labels" and the values in the table are all right-aligned by default.)

Also, a quick note: if the PivotTable Fields task pane ever disappears on you, just click onto your PivotTable to bring it back. (If you're not actively working in the PivotTable that task pane as well as the extra PivotTable Tools tabs at the top go away.)

Pivot Table With Multiple Criteria In Rows and Columns

Now let's move on to a third, more complex example that has multiple criteria in both the rows and columns of the table. Here are the first few rows from the data we're going to use:

	A	B	C	E	F	G	H	I
1	**Month**	**Year**	**Title**	**Author Name**	**Quantity**	**Royalty**	**Ad Cost**	**P or L**
2	January	2015	Title A	Author A	0.00	$0.00		$0.00
3	January	2015	Title C	Author C	84.00	$108.82		$108.82
4	January	2015	Title D	Author C	23.00	$33.74		$33.74

And here is the first portion of the PivotTable created with that data:

	A	B	C	D	E	F
1						
2						
3	Sum of P or L	Column Labels ▾				
4		⊟ 2015				
5	Row Labels ▾	January	February	March	April	May
6	⊟ Author A	$0.00	$6.23	$11.76	$4.80	$6.79
7	Title A	$0.00	$6.23	$11.76	$4.80	$6.79
8	⊟ Author B		$0.52			
9	Title B		$0.52			
10	⊟ Author C	$142.56	$59.69	$26.81	$10.83	
11	Title C	$108.82	$28.07	$9.36	$5.41	
12	Title D	$33.74	$20.37	$9.43	$2.71	
13	Title E		$11.25	$8.02	$2.71	
14	⊟ (blank)					
15	(blank)					
16	Grand Total	$142.56	$66.44	$38.57	$15.63	$6.79

The columns section has year and then month. The rows section has Author and then Title. It's important if you're going to use multiple parameters that you get them in the right order in the PivotFields section or else your data can get very ugly very fast.

Here is what that looks like for this table:

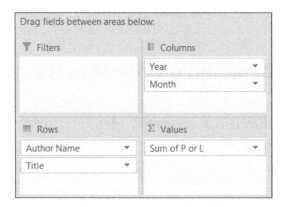

You can see that I have Year above Month and Author above Title. That sets the display order in the PivotTable so that all of the months for a specific year are listed first and then all of the months for the next year. Same with all of the titles for a specific author before the titles for the next author are listed.

If your data is displaying in the wrong order. Say, for example, I had Month above Year in that Columns section which would put all of January's results for every year first and then all of February's results for every year next, etc., it's a simple matter of clicking and dragging one of the fields into the correct order.

The table will update immediately with your changes so you can quickly see if you got it right.

One more note on this. Using multiple fields does not always work well. I almost always avoid using multiple fields in the Values section if I have more than one field in the Columns section. It just gets too busy to read easily.

Remove a Field

Another tip that we haven't talked about yet is what to do if you've placed a field into Filters, Columns, Rows, or Values and you decide you don't want it there.

One option is to click on the field name and choose Remove Field from the dropdown menu. Another is to uncheck the box next to the field name in the choose fields section. (That only works if you want to remove all uses of the field or if it was just used a single time.) You can also right-click on the field in the table itself and choose the Remove option from the dropdown there.

Hide Second-Level Data

Another thing you can do if you have multiple levels of data is hide the details from the second level of data so that you only see the summary values that pertain to the first level of data. You can do this on a case-by-case basis.

So in this data set we actually have data for 2015, 2016, 2017, 2018, 2019, and 2020.

2015 was not a very exciting year and it was a while ago. So maybe I don't care about seeing month-by-month data for that particular year.

I can click on the small negative sign next to 2015 and that will hide the monthly data for 2015 and just give me summary results. like so:

Sum of P or L	Column Labels		
	⊞2015	⊟2016	
Row Labels		January	February
⊟Author A	$51.09	$3.47	$2.98
Title A	$51.09	$3.47	$2.98
⊟Author B	$1.87		

Note that the minus sign is now a plus sign. To bring back the more detailed results, you just click on that + sign.

I could do the same on the left-hand side with Author so that I'm only seeing summary results at the Author level instead of the Title level.

To collapse all of the results at once instead of one-by-one, you can click into a cell in that row or column, right-click, and choose Collapse Entire Field.

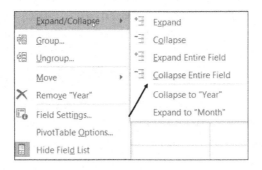

To expand it again, right-click and choose Expand Entire Field. Three's also an option to Expand or Collapse to a named level, "Year" or "Month", for example, which would come in useful if you had three levels of data in a row or column.

Grouping and Ungrouping

Another thing you can do in a PivotTable that I use somewhat often is group different selections.

For example, I have published audiobooks through two different distributors, ACX and Authors Republic. When I pull in my sales data it comes in under those two names. But sometimes when I'm generating summary reports I just want to look at overall audiobook numbers rather than specific numbers for each of those distributors.

There's no way for Excel to know that those two belong together without my somehow telling it that I want them grouped. (I could add a column to my data that puts them in an audiobook group, but since I haven't done that...)

To group two of the values in a column or row, highlight the labels of the rows or columns you want to group.

(They do not need to be next to one another. If they aren't you can use the Ctrl key as you select each one.)

Next, right-click and selected Group from the dropdown menu or go to the PivotTable Tools Analyze tab and choose Group Selection from there.

The entries you chose to group will now be next to one another and your data will have another level to it.

The group you created will be labeled Group 1, the rest of the entries at the new level will be labeled identically to their prior name.

Like so where I have chosen to Group Author A and Author C and they are now in Group 1 but Author B was left by itself so is now in a group labeled Author B:

Row Labels	
⊟ Group1	142.56
⊞ Author A	0
⊞ Author C	142.56
⊟ Author B	
⊞ Author B	
⊞ (blank)	
Grand Total	142.56

You can change the group name by clicking on the cell with the group name in it and then using the formula bar to type in the new name. Hit enter when you're done.

To ungroup values, click on a group name, right-click, and choose ungroup. This will remove all groupings at that level. You can also use the Ungroup option in the Analyze tab of the PivotTable Tools.

PivotTable Tools Analyze Tab

We've covered a lot so far and that's most of what I do in PivotTables, but there is a handy dandy Analyze tab under PivotTable Tools that's at least worth a quick look. Some of it we discussed already, like Refresh and Group/Ungroup, but let's walk through a few more of your options.

I'm going to do these in order of what I use rather than in order withing the tab so that if you start to get bored reading through this section you can just skip to the next section.

Fields, Items, & Sets

In addition to the calculations we already discussed, Excel allows you to add calculated fields to your table that combine more than one of the fields in your table to create a new value.

For example, let's say that I want to know my profit or loss per unit for my titles. I have a field that tells me units sold, Quantity, and I have a field that tells me total Profit and Loss, P or L. I can use the Calculated Field option under Fields, Items, & Sets to have Excel calculate P or L divided by Quantity for me with the data in the PivotTable.

Why do it this way instead of doing it in the source data table? Because in the source data we haven't aggregated our results. So I could calculate for every month what the profit or loss per unit was for a specific title and then take the average of those values, but I couldn't calculate the overall number since my data isn't aggregated until I do so through the PivotTable.

Let's walk through how to do that. Here's what we're going to start with. I've changed the column names, formatted the values, and filtered this to just 2015 data. (Note that when I changed the column name it also changed the name in the PivotTable Fields task pane so be aware that happens.)

Year	2015	
Row Labels	**Units**	**Profit**
− **Author A**	27	$51.09
Title A	27	$51.09
− **Author B**	2	$1.87
Title B	2	$1.87
− **Author C**	405	$298.73
Title C	263	$162.84
Title D	86	$90.14
Title E	55	$45.75
Grand Total	434	$351.69

Click on the PivotTable and then go to the Analyze tab under PivotTable Tools.

In the Calculations section click on the dropdown for Fields, Items, & Sets and choose Calculated Field.

You'll then see the Inert Calculated Field dialogue box.

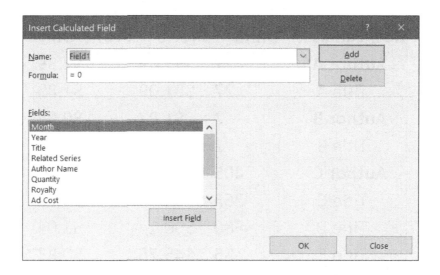

Under Name, type the name you want to use for the field.

Under Formula you need to type in a formula that will do your calculation. (We covered basic math operators in *Excel 2019 Beginner*. Use a plus sign for addition, minus sign for subtraction, asterisk for multiplication, and forward slash for division. If you want to do something more than that then look to *Excel 2019 Formulas and Functions* or use the Help function in Excel.)

You can click on the field names you need as you build your formula. They will be the original field names. So I clicked into that Formula box, left the = sign, deleted the 0, clicked on P or L, then typed a forward slash, then clicked on Quantity.

When you're done, click on Add. And then click on OK. Excel should add the new calculated field into your PivotTable. (If you don't click Add it may just add it to the list of available fields in the PivotTable Fields task pane.)

You can then format the new value like you would any other either in the PivotTable Fields task pane or the PivotTable cells themselves.

Because this was a summary table, Excel named the field in the table Sum of Profit Per Unit but what it's actually calculating is Profit divided by Units. So I'm going to ahead and rename it in my table but I have to tweak the name a bit because Excel won't let me use Profit Per Unit since that was the original name I used.

Here's what I end up with. A table that now has a third column Profit/Unit which is calculated based upon the values in two other cells in my table.

Year	2015		
Row Labels	**Units**	**Profit**	**Profit/Unit**
⊟**Author A**	27	$51.09	$1.89
Title A	27	$51.09	$1.89
⊟**Author B**	2	$1.87	$0.94
Title B	2	$1.87	$0.94
⊟**Author C**	405	$298.73	$0.74
Title C	263	$162.84	$0.62
Title D	86	$90.14	$1.04
Title E	55	$45.75	$0.83
Grand Total	434	$351.69	$0.81

The nice thing about using calculated values is they adjust as you move the table around. I could have done this same calculation off to the side of the table for one row but it would've stayed in place if/when I updated the table and may not have lined up anymore to the correct row in the table.

Which reminds me that there is an issue if you do calculations outside of a PivotTable that use values in a PivotTable: The calculations do not move with the PivotTable. The cell references the calculation uses are basically the set of rules that build that specific value in the PivotTable.

It sounds confusing. Let me show you.

If I use the values in this PivotTable to divide the value in C5 (which is $51.09) by the value in B5 (which is 27 units), the formula Excel creates looks like this:

=GETPIVOTDATA("Profit",A4,"Author Name","Author A")/
GETPIVOTDATA("Units",A4,"Author Name","Author A")

That is very different from the formula it would create if this weren't a PivotTable. If this weren't a PivotTable it would be =C5/B5.

That difference means that even as the table is updated and values move around, this calculation will continue to use the values for profit and units for Author A.

The way the calculation is structured makes it impossible to quickly create and copy a formula that references cells in a Pivot Table. You have to create the calculation one row at a time. (Or use a calculated field in the table like we just did, or do what I often do which is build the table, copy and paste special to turn it back into only values and then do the extra calculation.)

Okay. On to the next one.

Change Data Source

Change Data Source can be found in the Data section of the Analyze tab. It allows you to change the data that is being used in your current PivotTable.

Even when I use the top left corner of a worksheet to tell Excel to Select All of my data to build a PivotTable what Excel actually does is finds the limits of my existing data and defines the data range to use that way.

So, for example, with the latest data set we were working with, Excel gave the data range as 'Pivot Table Data 3'!$A:$I.

That's saying that the data in use was coming from a worksheet named Pivot Table Data 3 and Columns A through I of that worksheet. But what happens if I add on more data into Column J? Or Column K?

Excel will not automatically pick up that new data. If I don't want to start over with a new PivotTable, I have to go in and change the data source instead.

To do so, go to the Analyze tab, click on Change Data Source and then Change Data Source again in the dropdown menu.

That will open a Change PivotTable Data Source dialogue box.

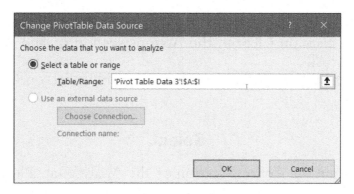

In this case, if I just wanted to change the range to include Column J, I could quickly click into that box and replace the I with a J and then click on OK. Once I did that my new field name would appear in the PivotTable Fields task pane

Another option is to use the backspace key to delete the current range, and then select your whole data range again.

Whatever you do, do not click into that space and try to use the arrow keys. If you do that, click cancel and try again. (When you use the arrow keys you're actually moving your cursor around within the data set and Excel is updating the data range to use but it's doing it one cell at a time. You could fix this by arrowing to the edge of your data set and then using the shift key as you select the rest of your data, but I find it easier to never go down that road in the first place.)

Refresh

We already discussed that you can use the Refresh option in the Data section of the Analyze tab to update the data in your table in case a change was made in the data set that Excel was pulling from.

I'm just going to make one more point here, which is that if you generate your PivotTable and find that there's an issue, for example, customer Albert Jones was entered as Albert Jones and Albert R. Jones, it's better to update the source data for your table than to try to manually fix it within the PivotTable. Manually fixing it fixes it just that one time. Updating it in the source data fixes it for life.

(Of course, in that kind of situation I would recommend having the raw data somewhere that you never ever touch and then the working data stored somewhere that you can fix. Just document what you've done.)

Clear

If you want to keep the PivotTable but start over fresh by removing all fields and settings, you can click on Clear in the Actions section of the Analyze tab, and then choose Clear All

To clear just the filters you've applied to the table, click on Clear and choose Clear Filters.

Select

The Select option in the Actions section of the Analyze tab allows you to Select the entire PivotTable, just the labels, or just the values. Click on Select to see the dropdown menu of your options.

Initially your only choice will be Entire PivotTable which will highlight all of the cells in the table, including any filters.

You can then choose Labels or Values from the dropdown and it will confine your selection to just the labels in the table or the values in the table. (There is also a Labels and Values option but that appears to be the same as Entire PivotTable.)

If you had a PivotTable on a worksheet with a bunch of other information and just wanted to copy that PivotTable, this option would let you do that.

Move PivotTable

The Move PivotTable option in the Actions section of the Analyze tab allows you to move your entire PivotTable to a new worksheet or another location in the current worksheet. This is useful when you have other data in the worksheet and want to just move the PivotTable.

(When I was playing around with all of this I couldn't insert rows because of a PivotTable in an existing worksheet and used Move PivotTable to put that table elsewhere.)

Insert Slicer

Insert Slicer basically works like a filter except that the criteria you can choose from are visible on the screen in a separate dialogue box.

To insert a Slicer go to the Analyze tab under PivotTable Tools and choose Insert Slicer from the Filter section. That will bring up a list of your available fields, click on one and a slicer will appear on the screen that lists all of the values for that field.

Year	2015			Title		
				Title A		
Row Labels	Units	Profit	Profit/Unit	Title B		
Author B	2	$1.87	$0.94	Title C		
Title B	2	$1.87	$0.94			
Grand Total	2	$1.87	$0.94	Title D		
				Title E		
				(blank)		

Here I've created a Slicer for Title and then selected just Title B. You can see that the PivotTable updated to show that.

To select more than one field you can use the shift or control keys or you can click on the multi-select option at the top. It's the list with the checkmarks next to each line. After you select that, you can click on all the fields you want without needing to use Ctrl or shift. If you use multi-select, click on it again to turn it off.

To clear your selection, click on the funnel image in the top right corner of the slicer box or use Alt + C. (You may have to click on it more than once depending on where you were before you tried to click on it.)

You can also have more than one slicer open at once.

When you have a slicer open and are clicked onto it, there will be a Slicer Tools Options tab available that lets you format the slicer and determine its position on the page.

Slicers can be useful if you want to filter your data by more than one value and want to see what values you've chosen since in that case the standard Filter option would just show Multiple.

It can also come in handy if you are giving access to the PivotTable to other users and you want them to be able to click on the available choices without having to use a Filter dropdown.

To remove a slicer, click on it and then hit the delete key.

Insert Timeline

Insert Timeline works with date fields and lets you narrow down your results by month, quarter, year, or day.

This is very handy for data where you have just the date (8/9/15) but want to see the data by month or year without having to add new fields to your original data source. (And certainly beats my old method of filtering by date and then checking/unchecking boxes.)

Here is a timeline from our second data set which included Date of Sale:

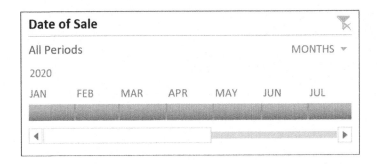

You can either click on those individual months to see the data for a specific month or that dropdown on the right can be changed to show years, quarters, or days instead.

I have at times found Excel didn't want to acknowledge a field as a valid date field, but when it does, using the timeline is very helpful

* * *

Alright.

Hopefully that was a good, solid beginning with respect to pivot tables. If you want to go further with them, your best bet is the Microsoft help options.

Charts – Discussion of Types

Charts are a great way to visualize your data. They take a big pile of numbers and turn them into a pretty picture. And, like they say, a picture is worth a thousand words.

I'm pretty good at recognizing patterns if you let me skim an entire data set, but a chart can show what I feel is true (such as that a large percent of sales are coming from one source) with just a few clicks and a big block of color.

Data Format

First things first, your data needs to be arranged properly to create a chart.

Specifically, for most of the charts we're going to discuss, you need one set of labels across the top and one set down the side with values listed in the cells where those two intersect. Do not include subtotals if you can avoid it (you'll have to select around them if you do) and same with grand totals (you'll have to leave them out when you choose your cells). Also, don't include anything in the top left corner of the table where the row labels and column labels intersect.

Here are two examples which would work equally well for this data set.

DATA TABLE OPTION 1						
	201701	201702	201703	201704	201705	201706
Amazon	$100.00	$107.00	$114.49	$122.50	$131.08	$140.26
Createspace	$37.00	$39.59	$42.36	$45.33	$48.50	$51.89
ACX	$23.50	$25.15	$26.91	$28.79	$30.80	$32.96
Con Sales	$10.00			$25.00		$8.00

DATA TABLE OPTION 2				
	Amazon	Createspace	ACX	Con Sales
201701	$100.00	$37.00	$23.50	$10.00
201702	$107.00	$39.59	$25.15	
201703	$114.49	$42.36	$26.91	
201704	$122.50	$45.33	$28.79	$25.00
201705	$131.08	$48.50	$30.80	
201706	$140.26	$51.89	$32.96	$8.00

This is fictitious sales data for each month for various sales platforms. In the first example, the sales channels are listed down the side and the months are listed along the top with the intersection of those two showing the dollar value of sales for that sales channel for that period.

In the second example, each month is listed down the side and each of the sales channels is listed across the top.

How you format your data can impact how your data appears in your charts, especially if you add in a data table which we'll discuss later, so I highly recommend formatting the data in your source table. For example, when looking at my revenue numbers, I don't need to see the cents portion of the value so I usually format my currency entries to remove that.

Alright.

Let's walk through the basics of creating a chart and then we'll discuss the different chart options and what they look like.

Create a Chart

To create a chart from your data, highlight the cells that contain your labels and your values. Remember, do not include any subtotal rows or grand total rows.

If your data is not connected, so you can't just select a single range of values, you can use the Ctrl key to select non-continuous rows or columns.

To do this, select your first range, hold down the Ctrl key, and select your second range. Continue on doing so until all of your data is selected.

Just be sure that each of the selected ranges has the same number of rows or columns so that if they were put together they would form a table with an even number of rows and columns

(The reason this matters is for data integrity, because there's no way to know in your chart whether you're missing results for a particular combination of criteria because it doesn't exist or because you simply didn't select the proper cells. Both will look the exact same in your chart.)

Once you have your data selected, go to the Charts section of the Insert tab and click on the dropdown menu for the chart type you want, and then choose your chart from there. The chart will appear in a new window on top of your worksheet.

Clicking on Recommended Charts in that same section will bring up the Insert Chart dialogue box.

Clicking over to All Charts will show you every available chart type Excel has to offer, listed by category.

If you've selected a set of data that Excel understands (i.e., connected rows and columns) then when you click on Recommended Charts the Recommended Charts tab in the Insert Chart dialogue box will show a handful of charts that Excel thinks match your data. Like this example for our data table on the last page.

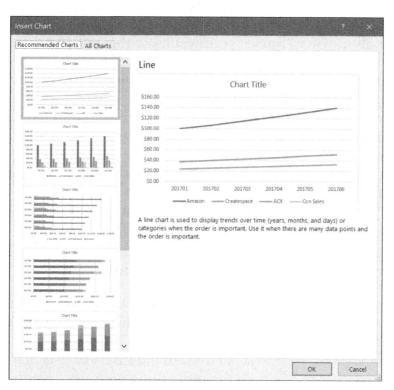

This can be a convenient starting point if you're not sure how you want to display your data. (We will walk through the most common types of charts in a moment after we finish discussing how to create a chart.)

If you're not sure what chart you want, in the Charts section of the Insert tab if you hold your mouse over each chart selection the chart will appear in a separate window so you can easily tell whether it's what you want before you make your selection. But you need to actually click on your selection for it to stay.

Which Chart To Choose

The general rule when choosing a chart is that for time series data like the examples above that include multiple variables (your sales channels) across multiple time periods (each month), the best choices are column charts, bar charts, and line charts.

For data where you have multiple variables but no time component (like total sales for the year), a better choice is a pie or doughnut chart.

Scatter charts are good for random data points where you're looking at the intersection of two or three variables to see if there's any sort of relationship between them.

Histograms allow you to bucket your results so that you can look at how many results you have in a specific range of values. This can often let you see a normal distribution of results, for example, where the majority of the values fall in the center with outliers in either direction.

Excel does offer additional chart types like treemaps, sunbursts, bubble charts and radar charts, but we're not going to cover them in this guide. If you need a chart like that you'll know how it works in general and hopefully our walkthrough of the most common chart types here will let you figure out how to create what you need.

Okay then. Time to discuss Column Charts, Bar Charts, Line Charts, Pie and Doughnut Charts, Scatter Charts, and Histograms in more detail.

Column and Bar Charts

Excel has switched things up a bit for Excel 2019 and now column charts and bar charts are combined under one dropdown in the Charts section of the Insert tab.

(Previously they were treated separately. In the Insert Charts dialogue box they still are. But since they're basically the same thing with the exception that one is horizontal and one is vertical, it kind of makes sense to combine them.)

To create a column or bar chart highlight your data, go to the Charts section of the Insert tab, and click on the dropdown arrow for the top left chart option.

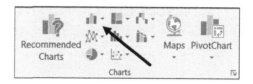

You will then see a dropdown menu with a series of choices. The first two sections are for column charts, the second two sections are for bar charts.

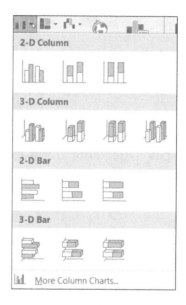

We're going to ignore the 3-D options. They're basically the exact same as the 2-D options just with that three dimensionality (which honestly, truly is probably not needed outside of consulting presentations or annual reports.)

The final 3-D option is a more advanced chart type that creates a three-variable graph, and we're not going to cover that in this guide. (Consider it an Advanced Excel Topic.)

With column and bar charts Excel gives you three choices of chart type. You can choose from clustered, stacked, and 100% stacked.

The clustered option puts the results for each variable (sales platform in the below example) side-by-side for each observation (month in the below example).

You can easily see the height difference between different results, but it can quickly become too busy if you're dealing with a large number of variables.

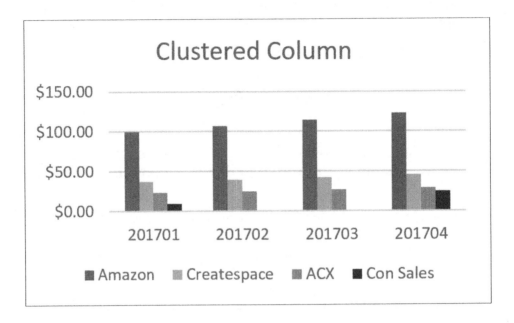

The bar chart version is basically the same thing except the bars are horizontal instead of vertical. The observations move from bottom to top instead of from right to left like in the column chart.

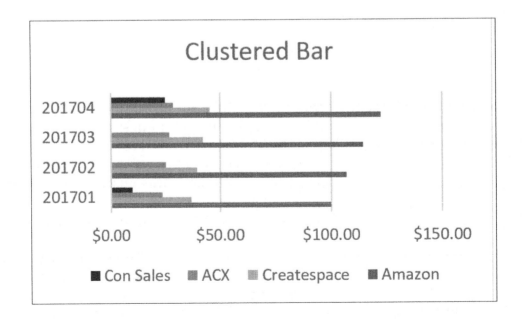

When you have a large number of variables, like I do with my sales channels, then the stacked option is a better choice.

Like with the clustered option, the stacked option has bars of different sizes for each variable based on their value relative to the other values in the chart, but this time the bars are stacked one atop the other instead of shown side-by-side.

So you end up with only one column or bar per time period but you can still identify which one is the largest value based upon the portion of the column or bar it takes up. Like in this Stacked Column chart where Amazon clearly dominates:

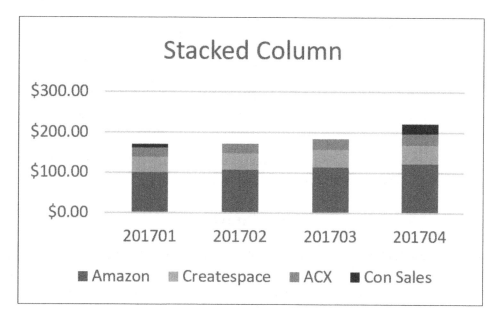

The stacked option is good for showing the overall change from time period to time period.

The 100% stacked option presents all of the information in one column just like the stacked option does. But instead of basing each section's height on its value, it shows the percentage share of the whole which means every single column or bar is the exact same height (which represents 100%).

While you lose any measurement of value (a column chart with values of 2:5:5 will look the exact same as one with values of 20:50:50 or 200:500:500), you can better see changes in percentage share for each variable. (A variable that goes from 10% share to 50% share will be obvious.)

This is an example of the same data as above but in a 100% Stacked Column chart.

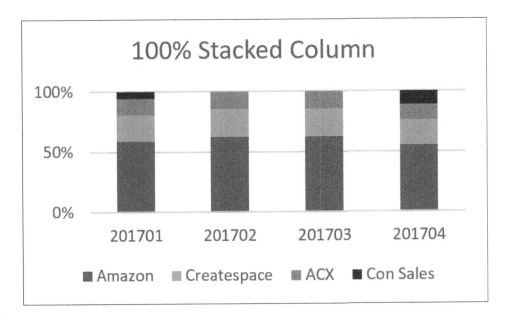

The stacked and 100% stacked bar charts are basically the same as the column chart equivalents except the bars are horizontal instead of vertical.

Line Charts

Line charts are the first chart type shown in the second row of choices. In Excel 2019 they have been combined with area charts, which we're not going to cover.

We're also not covering the 3-D options. And I'm actually only going to cover two of the six 2-D options.

(The other four are meant to do what the stacked columns graphs do and show relative values. I have seen them used by epidemiologists this year to explain data, but I think they're generally counterintuitive unless set up properly with shading under each line.)

So for our purposes all we want are Line and Line with Markers which are the first and the fourth choices.

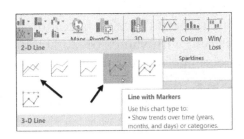

The difference between the line chart and line chart with markers is basically whether there is a point on the line for each observation or not.

Here they are for our data set where we've chosen to chart amount earned per period for four time periods for our four sales channels.

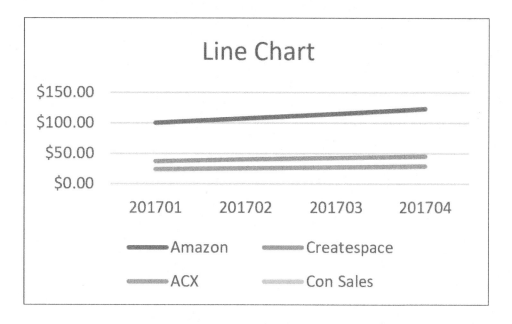

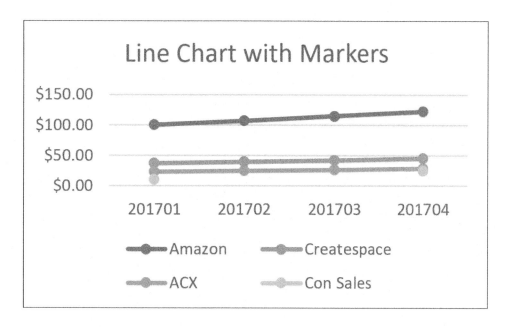

Alright, so that covered the three primary options when dealing with time-series data. But what about data that is all for one time period. For example, sales in a given month or in a given year. That's when the next chart types can be used.

Pie and Doughnut Charts

Pie and doughnut charts are best used when you have one set of observations and want to see the share of the total for each value.

The pie and doughnut chart option is at the bottom on the left-hand side of the chart options. In the dropdown you'll see one 3-D choice as well, but we're just going to use the 2-D ones.

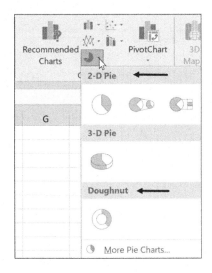

For the pie charts, you can choose between a standard pie chart, a pie of pie chart, or a bar of pie chart. The doughnut chart just has the one option which is the equivalent of the basic pie chart.

If you're only focused on who or what accounts for the biggest share, then use the standard pie chart or the doughnut chart. Each one will assign a section based on relative value for that category. (So share of sales for the period for each sales channel, for example, where the circle is equal to 100%.)

If you want to be able to clearly see the results for all of your segments, even the smallest ones, then the pie of pie chart or the bar of pie chart are potentially better choices. (Although I'm not a fan of either one, to be honest.)

Now let's look at examples. I've used the 201701 data to build each of these.

Here are the basic pie and doughnut chart:

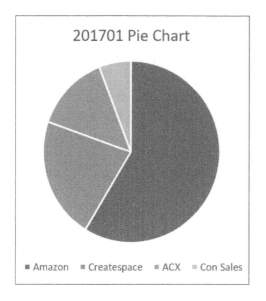 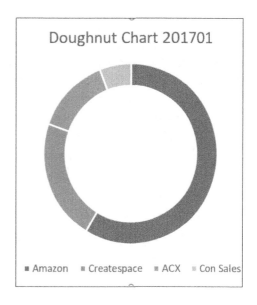

Each chart took the values for a channel (Amazon, CreateSpace, ACX, Con Sales) and assigned it a slice of the pie or circle based upon its relative share ($100, $37, $23.50, and $10) of the whole.

The only difference between the two is that a doughnut chart is hollow in the center.

Now on to the pie of pie charts and the bar of pie chart. Here is an example of a pie of pie chart:

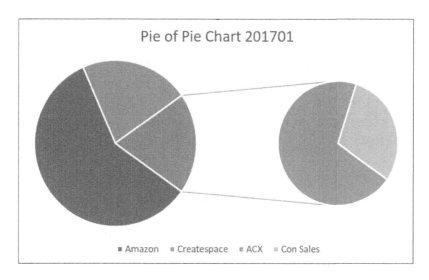

The pie of pie chart creates one main pie chart in which it combines the smaller results to form one segment. Those smaller results are then broken out into another pie chart of their own.

So in the chart above we have ACX and Con Sales that are represented in the main pie chart as one "slice" alongside the other two slices for Amazon and CreateSpace. Those two channels, ACX and Con Sales, are then broken out in their own pie chart on the right-hand side where the size of the slices is base don their value relative to one another. So even though they only represent about 20% of the total between them and Con Sales are only 1/10 of Amazon sales that's not obvious from the way this data is displayed.

The bar of pie chart does the same except it breaks out the smaller results into a stacked bar chart like so:

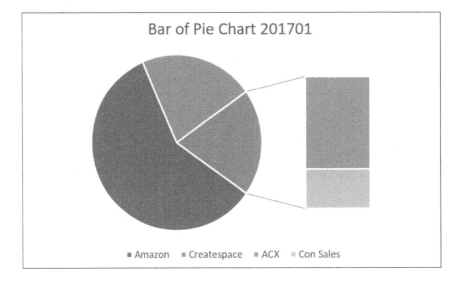

In order to avoid confusion I think the bar of pie chart is probably the better choice of the two since it more clearly distinguishes that it's a subset of data, but honestly I wouldn't use either one if I could avoid it.

(The best charts can be read without explanation and I'm not sure that would be true for either the pie of pie chart or the bar of pie chart for your average user.)

Scatter Charts

Scatter charts (or scatter plots) are the second option on the bottom row of the chart types.

Scatter charts plot the value of variable A given a value for variable B. For example, if I were trying to figure out if gravity is a constant, I might plot how long it takes for a ball to reach the ground when I drop it from varying heights. So I'd plot time vs. distance. From that I could eventually see that the results form a pattern which does indicate a constant. (Thanks high school physics teacher for making physics fun.)

There are five scatter plot options.

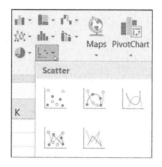

The first one is a classic scatter plot. It takes variable A and plots it against variable B, creating a standalone data point for each observation. It doesn't care what order your entries are in, because there's no attempt to connect those entries to form a pattern.

Here we have some sample height and time values that we've plotted using that first Scatter option. There is a clear pattern to the data that will be much more obvious if we change the chart type to connect those points.

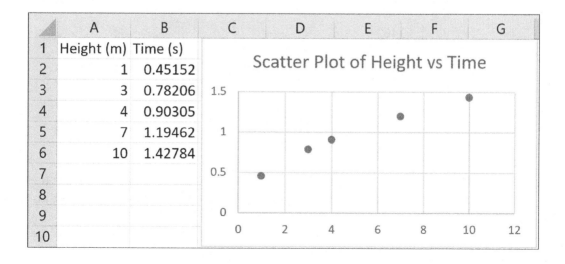

That's where the other four scatter plot options comes into play. They all include lines drawn through the plotted points.

The two smooth line options try to draw the best curved line between points. The straight line options just connect point 1 to point 2 to point 3 using straight lines between each point.

The charts with markers show each of the data points on the line, the charts without markers do not.

Now. One quirk of Excel is that it draws the line from the first set of coordinates in the data table to the next set of coordinates.

This introduces another factor into the table since the order of your data impacts the appearance of your chart.

If the order in which you recorded your observations does not matter, like in this example where it doesn't matter if I drop a ball from 1 meter or 10 meters first, then you should sort your data before plotting it.

In the chart above, because there were no lines to connect the dots whether the data was sorted or not didn't matter. But here's that same data in random order and with a smooth line connecting the data points.

This one has markers so you can still see the curve in the underlying data, but if I were to take those out it would just look like a giant scribble on the page.

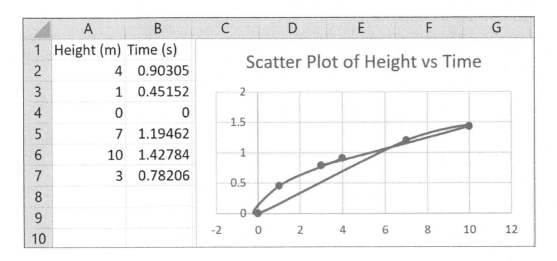

Here is that same data now sorted by height. (I could have as easily sorted by time.) I've used the same plot type of smooth line with markers so you can see the difference.

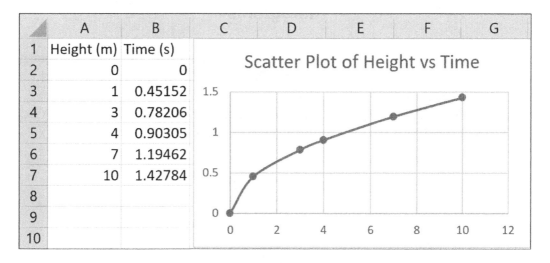

Okay. That was an example with just two data points in it. But you can map multiple sets of data in a basic scatter plot by adding another column of data. The first column will serve as your control value and then the next two columns are the values you're plotting against the control values.

For example, let's say you have sales numbers for two car sales representatives for the first four months of the year and want to compare them to one another.

Here is our data as well as a scatter line plot with straight lines and no markers.

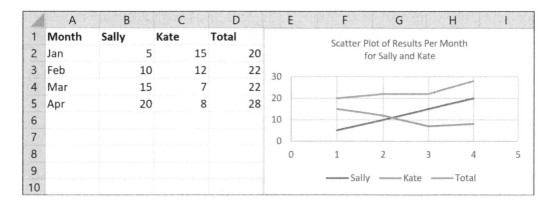

The lines let you clearly see the trend for each of the three categories. Sally is doing better each month, Kate has been doing worse. For the total between them there was a slight increase in the last month measured.

You can technically do a plot like this without plot lines. Each data point will be color-coded, but I don't recommend doing so. It's not near as easy to interpret as the versions with lines connecting related observations.

Histograms

On to one I didn't cover in the original *Intermediate Excel* because it's relatively new but that I think is useful enough that we can cover it here. And that's histograms.

In Excel 2019 the histogram option is located under the center chart choice, Insert Statistic Chart. It is the top choice under that dropdown.

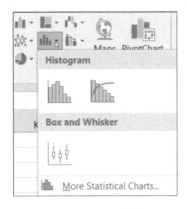

A histogram is perfect for seeing the general distribution of your data results. Rather than plot individual points what it does is buckets your values together into ranges called bins.

So, for example, instead of treating 31, 32, and 33 as separate values a histogram might have a bin for any value between 30 and 39. This can let you more easily see where your values cluster together without getting lost in the minutiae.

Here's our example. I've made up a series of high temperatures for January for a random location similar to Colorado.

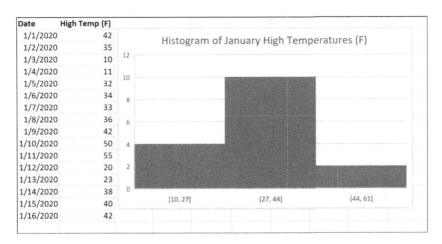

You can see that the range of values has been put in three bins by Excel and that the majority of the values fall into the center bin which contains all values between 27 and 44. The height of each bin is based upon how many values fall into the given range.

(We'll talk next about editing charts. In the chart formatting task pane for a histogram you can set the bin width and/or the number of bins.)

Okay?

Now that you understand the basic chart types, let's talk about how to edit your charts to get them to look exactly like what you want.

Charts - Editing

Chances are, once you've created a chart you'll want to edit it. With the sample charts I showed you in the last chapter I edited the name of each one, resized them, and moved them. But you can do much more than that and we're going to walk through a lot of those options now starting with the Chart Tools Design tab.

Chart Tools Design Tab

The Chart Tools Design tab is only available when you're clicked onto a chart. Once you do so the Chart Tools Design and Format tabs will appear to the right of the Help tab.

We're going to discuss the Design tab and the options on the right-hand side first because these are the ones you can use to fix a chart that doesn't seem to be working the way you expected it would.

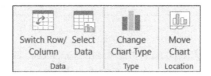

Those options are Switch Row/Column, Select Data, Change Chart Type, and Move Chart.

Switch Row/Column

Once you've created your chart you may find that the data you wanted along the bottom is along the side and the data you wanted along the side is along the bottom. Or even that the data you thought should be in the chart as the results isn't in the chart but is instead along one of the axes.

The first way I try to fix this is by click on Switch Row/Column data. Often that does it. (If that doesn't work then you'll need to consider whether you've selected the correct data and whether the chart type you're using is the right one.)

Select Data

If you realize that the data in your chart isn't what you wanted, you can either delete the chart and start over, which is sometimes the easiest choice if you've done nothing to customize the chart yet.

Or you can go to Select Data and change the data you've selected.

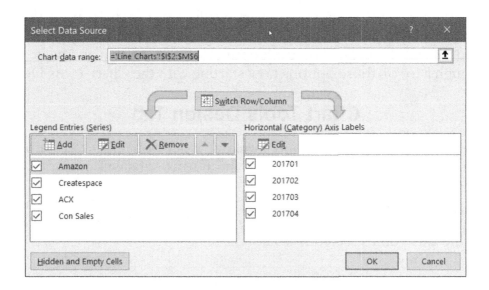

When you click on Select Data this will bring up the Select Data Source dialogue box. You can also see on the screen in the background the selected range of cells that are being used in your chart.

The chart data range at the top shows the selected cells that are being used in the chart. You can manually edit this by clicking into the box with the cell range or edit it by clicking on your worksheet and selecting a new range of cells there.

(I usually use another method for this, which is to click on my chart until I see my selected range of data highlighted and then to click and drag on the square that appears at the edge of the selected range until my new data is also selected.

On my screen those squares are purple, red, or blue and I usually want the purple one that is at the bottom of my left-hand labels. I click and drag down to add more rows of data to the range or drag up to remove rows from the range of data selected.)

If the problem is that you included a category you didn't want to include, like Grand Total, you can also just uncheck that category in the bottom section. For example, under Legend Entries for this table I could uncheck any of the sales channels to remove it from the chart or under Horizontal Axis Labels I could uncheck any of the date values to remove that date range from the chart.

To permanently remove one of the Legend Entries, select it and choose Remove. That will automatically update your data range above as well.

To add a series, you can also click on Add, give the series a name or click on the cell that contains that name already, and then in the series values field select the data to include from your worksheet.

To edit a series under Legend Entries, select the series you want to edit, click on Edit, and then change the selected cells or the name to what you want.

To change the order of the series elements, click on one of the elements and use the up and down arrows.

Change Chart Type

Sometimes you realize that the chart type you chose is the wrong one. Maybe you chose a stacked columns chart and realize that the 100% stacked columns chart is the better option. One way to change to the new chart is to click on Change Chart Type in the Chart Tools Design tab.

That will bring up the Change Chart Type dialogue box with the All Charts tab showing. If you're not sure what you want, you can see suggestions on the Recommended Charts tab that we talked about before. Or you can just select the chart you want from the All Charts tab.

(Another option is to go to the Insert tab and choose a new chart type from there. That will work, too.)

Move Chart

I will confess I never use this. But if you want to move a chart to a new worksheet you can click on that chart and then click on Move Chart and it will give you the option to move the chart to a new worksheet or an existing worksheet in the current workbook.

I usually just select the chart, copy or cut, go to the new location, and paste it.

(We'll talk in a few pages about how to move a chart around within a worksheet, but for now let's finish up with the Design tab.)

The left-hand side of the Design tab (below) is more about the appearance of the chart. I'm going to work from right to left because the left-most option will take an entire page or two to explain.

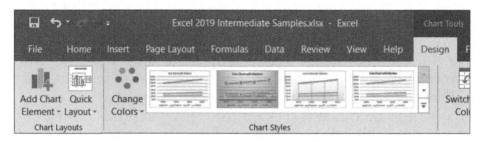

Chart Styles

Excel 2019 provides a number of pre-defined Chart Styles you can choose from.

The number of choices varies depending on the type of chart, but there are usually a variety with different colors and chart elements included or excluded.

In the screen shot above, you can see four examples for a line chart. On the left-hand side of those four options is a scroll bar that will allow you to see even more options.

If you want to see what a style will look like before you choose it, just hold your mouse over it and your chart will update to show the style. Once you find a style you like, click on it and Excel will apply that style to your chart.

I'd say that for me none of the chart styles are ever exactly what I want, but if one is close it can sometimes be easier to select it and then customize from there, especially if you're not quite sure what Chart Element that style is using that gives the chart the appearance you like.

Change Colors

I actually used this for a few of the chart screenshots in the last chapter because the default colors that Excel uses for charts are blue, orange, gray, and yellow and that doesn't always allow for the best contrast when looking at an image in black and white.

We'll talk later about how to change the colors for each item individually to exactly the color you want, but if what you're looking for is a quick and easy option for other color schemes, then Change Colors is the easiest way to get that.

First, click on Change Colors to see the dropdown menu of options. I count seventeen choices. The first few use a variety of colors, the rest use shades of one specific color.

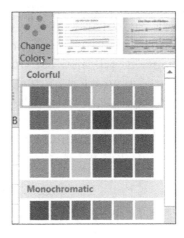

As with Chart Styles you can hover your mouse over each option to see what it will look like. When you find one you like, click on it and Excel will apply it to your chart.

Quick Layout

The Quick Layout dropdown provides a variety of layout options to choose from. The exact number will again depend on the chart type you've chosen.

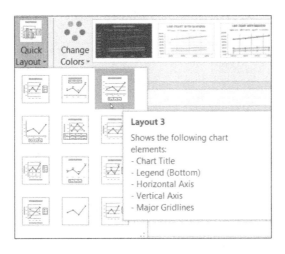

The layouts include various configurations of data labels, axes labels, legends, and grid lines. (One option for scatter charts even includes an r-squared calculation.)

To use a Quick Layout, click on the dropdown and choose the one you want.

Just like with the other quick formatting options, you can hover over each one to see what it will look like before you make your choice. When you do that, as you can see in the above image, it will also list out for you what the different formatting elements are that are being used in that Quick Layout.

If you use a Quick Layout after you choose a Chart Style the color scheme and background colors will stay the same as the Chart Style, but the layout will update. If you choose a Quick Layout and then a Chart Style, the Chart Style will override your Quick Layout, so if you want to combine the two start with your Chart Style.

Add Chart Element

This is the one I use the most. Because I almost always want a data table under my chart so that I can combine the visual chart with the actual results. But there are a lot of other options available here, too.

This is where you go to have more granular control over your axes, titles, data labels, etc.

The options available vary by chart type. If an option isn't available it will be grayed out. For example, Data Table, Lines, and Up/Down Bars are not available for scatter plots.

To see your choices, click on the Add Chart Element arrow. This will bring up a dropdown menu. You can then hold your mouse over each option in the list to see a secondary dropdown menu of available choices.

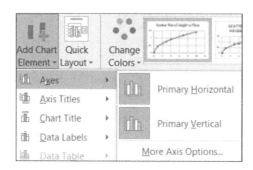

As above, holding your mouse over an option will show that choice on your chart, but you have to click on it to keep it.

If you click on the More Options choice at the bottom of one of those dropdown menus, that will bring up the chart formatting task pane on the right-hand side of the screen which will give you even more control over your charts.

We'll talk about the task pane in a bit. First, let's walk through the options in the Add Chart Element dropdown.

Axes

Axes allows you to add (or remove) the data point labels on each axis.

For example in this chart I clicked on Primary Vertical to remove the vertical axis values which were there by default.

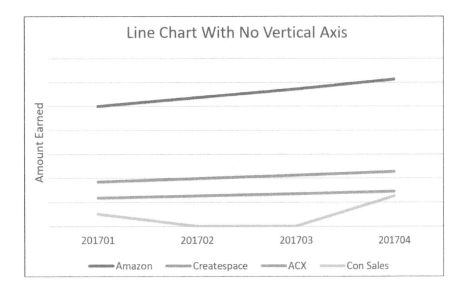

You can no longer see the $ values represented by each line on the chart. You just know that Amazon is much higher than the other lines but not by how much. This could be $5 compared to $1 or $5,000 compared to $1,000.

Axis Titles

Axis Titles allows you to add (or remove) a title for each axis.

In the image above I clicked on Primary Vertical to add a label to the vertical access. I then clicked into the box that was added and changed it to "Amount Earned". The chart above does not have a horizontal axis title.

Chart Title

Chart Title allows you to either (a) remove the chart title entirely, (b) place it at the top of the chart, or (c) place it in a centered overlay position.

All of the examples you've seen so far have the title above the chart.

Data Labels

You can use Data Labels to label each of the data points in your chart.

I find this particularly useful with pie charts and for those will usually choose the Outside End option or the Best Fit option, like below.

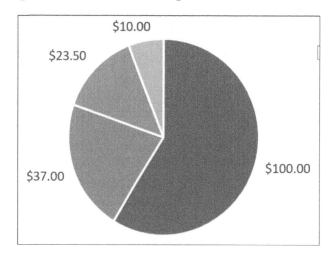

I do sometimes have to click on the labels and drag them to a better location. If you drag them far enough a line will appear connecting the label to its slice.

The default is to show the value, like above, but you can go into the task pane and make that into a percent share instead.

Data Table

Data Table allows you to add or remove a table below your chart that shows the data that was used to create it.

If you're going to do this, you should also at the same time consider removing the legend from the table since you can use the Data Table With Legend Keys option to combine the data table with a legend.

Below is an example of what this looks like with a 100% stacked column chart.

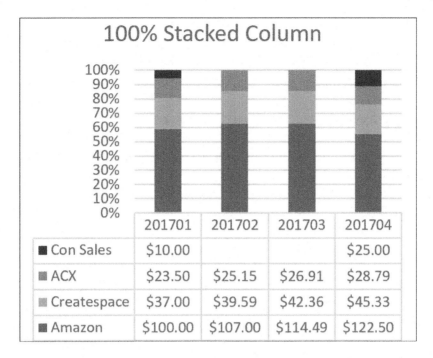

100% Stacked Column	201701	201702	201703	201704
■ Con Sales	$10.00			$25.00
■ ACX	$23.50	$25.15	$26.91	$28.79
■ Createspace	$37.00	$39.59	$42.36	$45.33
■ Amazon	$100.00	$107.00	$114.49	$122.50

When you add a data table you will likely have to resize the chart and make it taller to get it to look good. Otherwise it tends to get smooshed up into nothing.

In this example I have added a data table with legend keys, removed the legend that was there, and increased the overall height of the chart.

Error Bars

You can add bars that show the standard error, standard deviation, or percentage error in your data. (Usually you would use these if you had a data set that was predicting values and you wanted to show your potential error range. I wouldn't recommend using these on a chart unless you're dealing with data of that type and know what you're doing.)

Gridlines

The gridlines option allows you to add (or remove) horizontal or vertical lines to your chart. These can make it easier to identify the approximate value of a specific point in the chart. There are Primary Major Horizontal gridlines on the chart above.

Legend

The column, bar, line, pie, and doughnut charts that Excel creates come with a legend which is the listing of the categories in the chart and their corresponding color.

(For the charts we looked at earlier, those little boxes with Amazon, CreateSpace, etc. at the bottom were the legend.)

You can remove the legend using this dropdown like I did above, or you can change its position to right, left, top, or bottom.

If you choose top and bottom, the legend elements will be in a row. If you choose right or left, they'll be displayed in a column.

Lines

Lines allows you to add high-low lines or drop lines to a line chart.

Trendline

You can use Trendline to add a line onto your data to see if it fits a pattern like a linear or exponential relationship. Depending on the data set, you may be limited in your choice of lines you can add. Also, beware of using something like a linear trendline on exponential data. Excel will do it, but it's not the best fit for that sort of data.

Up/Down Bars

You can use this to add Up/Down bars to a line graph if you need them.

* * *

Now that you have all of the elements in place, time to discuss how to change the aesthetics of the chart. Things like size, position, and colors. Some of this you can do directly on the chart in the worksheet and some of it requires using the Chart Tools Format tab.

We'll start with a discussion of what you can do in the Chart Tools Format Tab.

Chart Tools Format Tab

Chart Size

You can go to the Size section on the right-hand side of the Format tab under Chart Tools and specify a width and height for your chart.

Be careful because it doesn't automatically adjust both dimensions. So if it matters that you keep your values proportional, calculate that before you make your change.

I usually use the Size option when I want multiple charts to be the exact same size. Otherwise, I actually change my chart size on the chart itself.

In Excel 2019, if you click onto a chart you've created you'll see white circles appear at each of the corners as well as in the middle of each side. Hover your mouse over each of them and you'll see that the cursor turns into a two sided arrow. If you don't see the two-sided arrow, click on one of the circles and hold your mouse over it again and it should work the second time.

Once you see the two-sided arrow, left-click and drag and you can increase or decrease the size of your chart. Click and drag from the corners to change both horizontal and vertical size at the same time.

With either method, all of the elements within the chart will resize themselves automatically to fit the new size.

Shape Styles

The easiest way to change the color of your chart elements like the bars in a bar chart or pie slices in a pie chart is to use Change Colors.

But if those colors aren't sufficient, you can use the Shape Styles section in the Format tab to change the color of each separate element in the chart one-by-one.

To do so, left-click on the element with the color you want to change. In a bar or column chart all sections that correspond to that category should be selected when you do that. If they aren't try double-clicking.

Also, be careful with pie charts because Excel likes to select all of the slices in the pie, not just that one. If that happens, click on the slice you want one more time and it should select just that slice.

Once you've chosen the element to change, you can click on one of the Shape Styles options which change the fill, outline, and text color. Or you can use the Shape Fill or the Shape Outline dropdown arrows to select a fill or outline color.

Use Shape Fill for bar, column, and pie graphs and Shape Outline for 2-D line graphs.

(If you ever create a 3-D line graph be careful, because if you use Shape Outline you'll only be changing the color on the edges of the line, not the entire line. For those you need to use both Shape Fill and Shape Outline.)

If you use one of the Shape Styles that will automatically be applied to your selected chart element as soon as you click on it. You can hover over each option to see what it will look like before you make your choice.

With Shape Fill or Shape Outline what you will see in the dropdown is a selection of colors as well as the ability to use a custom color with More Color.

With Shape Fill you can also use a picture, gradient, or texture. (Just don't go overboard on that, please. My little corporate soul cringes at the idea of how that could be abused to create truly hideous charts.)

With Shape Outline you can change the weight and type of line used. So you could have a dashed line instead of a solid line, for example.

If you don't like the result, remember to use Ctrl + Z to undo and try again.

There's another option in that section called Shape Effects that allows you to add things like beveling and shadows to the elements in your chart, but I'd encourage you to remember that the central purpose of a chart is to convey information to others and that sometimes adding a lot of bells and whistles gets in the way of that. But you do you.

WordArt Styles

For text in your chart you can apply fancy formatting to the text using the Word Art Styles options. Just select the text you want to format and then choose the WordArt Style you want.

You can also change the text color of text using the dropdown menu next to that which is called Text Fill. (The Home tab formatting options work as well but here you can also apply a picture, gradient, or texture instead of just a solid color.)

In the dropdown after that you can add lines of various widths or patterns around your letters. And in the dropdown after that you can add shadow, glow, reflection, etc. to your letters.

Please use sparingly. I know it's not my business but as someone who has been forced to sit through one too many garish presentations, I have to try.

Edits To Make Within A Chart

As mentioned above, there are some edits you can make directly in the chart. We already talked about changing the chart size that way. Now let's discuss a few other options you have.

Move a Chart

If you want to move a chart within your worksheet, left-click on an empty space within the chart, hold and drag. (You may have to click on the chart once and then click again and hold and drag.)

Don't click on an element within the chart, like the title, because that will just move that element around instead of the whole chart. If you do that, like I sometimes do, just Ctrl + Z to put the element back where it was and try again.

If you want to move a chart to another worksheet or even another file (including a Word file or PowerPoint presentation, for example), you can click onto an empty space within the chart and use Ctrl + C to copy it or Ctrl + X to cut it, and then go to the new destination and use Ctrl + V to paste it there.

Move Elements Within a Chart

You can manually move elements within a chart by left-clicking on the element and then clicking and dragging it to where you want it.

You should see a four-sided arrow when you are able to do this. For fields that can be edited or moved like the various title fields, this may require you to put the mouse along the edge of the field before you can click and drag to move.

Rename a Chart

To change the name of a newly-created chart, left-click on where it says Chart Title to select the title. You should see the title is now surrounded by a box with blue circles in each corner. Click into that box and highlight the existing text, delete it, and then add your own text.

If you're just editing an existing chart name you basically do the same. Click on it to see the box, click into the box, make your edits.

Rename a Data Field as Displayed in the Legend

To change the data labels used in the legend, your best bet is to do so in the data table that's the source of the data in the chart. As soon as you do that, the chart legend will update as well. I mention this here because it can be tempting to assume you can do those changes within the chart and you really can't.

Change Font Properties

If you want to change the font, font color, font size, or font style (italic, bold, underline), another option is to just click on the text element in the chart and then go to the Home tab and change the font options there just like you would with ordinary text in any cell.

Chart Formatting Task Pane

I've alluded to it a few times before, but you may have noticed as you work in your charts that sometimes on the right-hand side an extra box of options appears. This is what I refer to as the chart formatting task pane. There are actually a number of them that appear depending on the chart type and what you clicked on to make it appear.

For example, I'm looking at one labeled Format Plot Area right now. It has that name at the top but right under that is a dropdown menu where I can go to other task panes for that type of chart. Within each of these task panes there are then a few categories of changes that you can make and under each category there are subcategories to choose from that then let you make a series of choices about your chart layout.

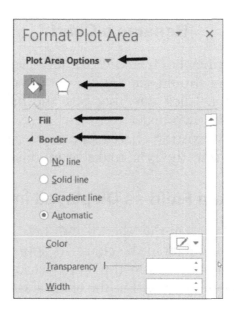

As mentioned before, you can open a task pane by choosing the more options choice for an element under Add Chart Element. Or you can double-click on your chart.

The options you'll be given vary depending on the type of chart and where you've clicked within that chart. You can do things like edit the fill style for chart elements, change the chart border, specify the size of the chart, choose how the text within the chart displays, etc. Basically, all of the things we've already discussed how to do elsewhere. But there are other options that you can only perform in the task pane as far as I know.

For a pie chart this is where I go to change the values shown on the data labels to percentages. (You have to have data labels added already and then it's Label Options, Label Options, and then click on Percentage and unclick Value under that second Label Options section.)

I also come here to "explode" my pie so that there is some space between the pie slices. (Pie explosion is in Series Options, Series Options, and then Series Options again. Move the slider under Pie Explosion to move the slices in the pie apart.)

For a histogram this is where I'd go to change the number of bins or the size of the bins. (Which is under Horizontal Axis, Axis Options, and then Axis Options again. Click on the buttons for what you want to change and the grayed-out values will become editable.)

Basically if there's something you want to do with a chart and you can't figure out where to do it, poke around in the chart formatting task pane.

* * *

Alright. That was charts. Lots and lots to cover, but now we're done and can move on to some much simpler topics.

Remove Duplicate Values

Sometimes I find myself with a data set that has values listed more than once, but all I really care about is the unique values. For example, you might have a listing of client transactions and want to extract from that a list of your client names. You don't need John Smith listed three times and going through and manually deleting those duplicate entries is painful.

Excel makes it very easy to remove duplicate entries using the Remove Duplicates option which is in the Data Tools section of the Data tab.

To get started, highlight the column(s) of data you're working with, go to the Data Tools section of the Data tab, and click on Remove Duplicates.

You'll then see the Remove Duplicates dialogue box which lets you choose which columns to remove duplicates from and also lets you indicate whether or not your data has headers.

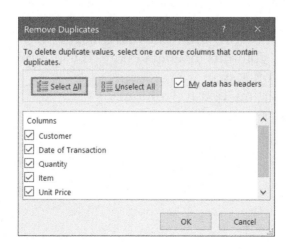

If you say that your data has headers, the first row of data will be excluded from the analysis.

Once you've made your selections, click OK.

You will then see a dialogue box from Excel telling you how many duplicates were found and removed and how many unique values remain.

With a single column selected, Remove Duplicates will return for you one instance of every unique entry in that column listed in continuous rows and all other data in that column will be deleted.

If you choose to remove duplicates from more than one column of data, Excel will consider the values in all of the selected columns when determining if a duplicate exists.

So if you remove duplicates from Columns A and B, Column A could have the same value listed more than once as long as it's paired with unique values in Column B.

Excel is looking for unique combinations of values between the two columns in that case.

It will then return values in the selected columns that are unique combinations of those values and delete extra rows.

If your selected a data range that had more columns than the ones you used to remove duplicates that means Excel may delete other data that wasn't unique. So if Column C had two values for one combination of Columns A and B, Excel only keeps one of them (and doesn't tell you it did that.)

This is a good point in time to repeat one of the key rules to data analysis: Keep your source data untouched. Always work with a copy. You never know when something you do will introduce an error and you won't realize it right away. You need that clean source data to go back to when that happens.

My recommendation on this is that you either use all of the columns in the range to remove duplicates or that you separate the column(s) you care about into a separate data set before you remove duplicates. Do not remove duplicates only using a subset of columns in a data range. It is not pretty. You will lose data that you don't know you lost.

Okay. On to Converting Text to Columns.

Convert Text to Columns

Converting text to columns allows you to take information that's all in one cell and split it out across multiple columns.

The most basic use of this is when you have something like comma-delimited data where all of the data is listed as one long entry with commas separating each piece of information, This happens with .csv files for example, although in modern versions of Excel, Excel does this for you automatically when it opens the file.

I also will use this as a trick to separate data if I just want one component of it or want to separate it into component parts.

For example, I was recently given a listing of employees where the entire employee name for each employee was in one cell with first name followed by last name. So "Bob Smith," "Alfred Jones," "Katie Clark," etc.

Because there was some variation in people's first names (Jim instead of James or a guy whose legal first name was Albert but who went by Dave), I wanted to change that list to one I could sort by last name.

Text to columns allowed me to easily do that by taking those name entries and splitting each one into one column for first name and one column for last name. I was then able to recombine the entries as Last Name, First Name.

Let's walk through how I did that first part:

Before you start make sure that there isn't any data in the columns to the right of the data you want to convert to columns because Excel will overwrite any existing data you have in those other columns when it separates out your values.

If you do have data in the columns to the right of the column you're converting, just insert columns to make space for the conversion. I'd recommend inserting a few more columns than you think you'll need.

(All it takes is one Alfred David Jones, Jr. in your list to create havoc.)

Next, highlight the cells with the data you want to convert, go to the Data tab, and in the Data Tools section click on Text to Columns.

This will bring up the Convert Text to Columns Wizard dialogue box which walks you through the conversion process.

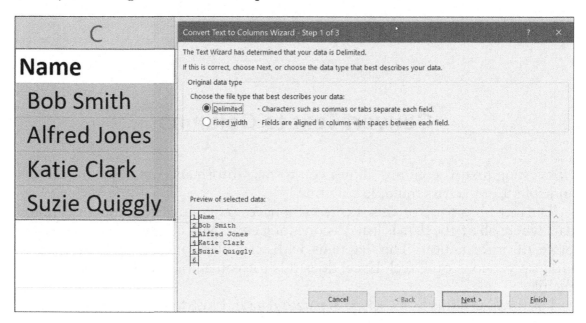

You have two options on the first screen: Delimited or Fixed Width.

Fixed Width lets you split your data into columns based upon number of characters/spaces without any consideration for what the actual content is.

Fixed Width conversion is useful when you have standardized entries that are all built the same way and you need to separate out a portion of those entries. For example, with a customer ID where the first three letters are a location identifier, you could use the fixed width option to separate the location portion of the identifier.

It's also nice because it doesn't require there to be a space or a comma or some other character like delimited does.

Delimited allows you to separate results of different lengths based upon the presence of a specified character or characters like a comma, a space, or a tab.

Once you've selected between Fixed Width and Delimited, click on Next.

This will take you to the second screen where you can set the break locations for Fixed Width or specify the delimiter(s) for Delimited. For both, the second screen has a preview section at the bottom that gives you an idea of what your results will look like.

For Fixed Width the lines you insert on the bottom will show where the data breaks. Breaks can be of any size. To insert a break line just click on the preview at the bottom. To delete it, double-click on the line you created. To move it, click on the line, hold that click and drag it to where you want it. As you drag it will look like a hatched line. When you release your click it will appear in the new location.

For Delimited you need to select at least one Delimiter.Below is the second screen for the Delimited option:

The top section has the available delimiters. These are where your breaks will occur, at each occurrence of the delimiter.

You can choose one or more of the listed options by clicking the checkboxes. You can also list a custom delimiter by using the Other box.

As you do so, the data preview section at the bottom will update to show how your data will be separated. Above I've chosen Space for my delimiter and you can see that there is a line showing between the first and last names where there's a space in my original data.

Any delimiters that you specify will be deleted from the final data. In this example, that means there will be no spaces left in either of the two columns that are going to be created.

On the third and final screen you can specify how each of your new columns should be formatted. If they don't need special formatting just click Finish on the second screen and you're done.

If they do need special formatting then click Next and select each column in the preview section of the third screen to specify your desired formatting (General, Text, Date, or do not import). Once that's done, click Finish.

You should now see that your entries have been split across multiple columns. In our example, "Bob Smith" in Column A becomes "Bob" in Column A and "Smith" in Column B. The space between the words is gone since that was our delimiter.

That scenario was pretty easy but not every scenario you'll encounter will be as simple.

For example, if the names in that list had been written as "Smith, Bob" instead, then I would've had to choose both commas and spaces as my delimiters. Otherwise, if I'd just chosen the comma as the delimiter it would have kept that space between the two words and I would've ended up with both a space and the word Bob in Column B. (If that ever happens to you, a quick fix is to use the TRIM function to trim the excess spaces around words.)

Some data is even more challenging to work with than that and requires multiple steps to convert.

For example, if you have "Smith, Bob, electrical engineer, Colorado" as your text string, you can't just specify space and comma as your delimiters. That would separate electrical engineer into two columns and you'd have significant issues if there were other work titles in your data that were shorter, like auditor, or longer, like senior vice president, because your data would no longer line up.

All Excel knows is what you tell it. If you tell it that spaces and commas are delimiters, that's what it does. It doesn't understand that that third entry is a title listing and that those words need to be kept together.

(In that scenario I'd separate using a comma and then TRIM the text to remove the excess spaces.)

As you can see from the above examples, it's important to always check your data after you convert it.

Limit Allowed Inputs Into A Cell

One of the biggest challenges with analyzing older data sets is that a lot of them didn't use standardized values. For example, one of the data sets I worked with started with paper forms that people completed by hand and that data was then input into a database exactly as it was written. Which meant that for a field like country you ended up with USA, U.S., Unites States, America, and all sorts of creative spellings of those words.

When that happens, it becomes an incredible challenge to do any sort of analysis on that data set. You can't just say, count all entries where country is United States, because you'll miss all those other entries. So then you have to create a list of all the possible variations that mean the same thing or you have to go through and standardize the data.

(Which I have seen backfire as well. That same data set had two separate questions that were merged into one in later forms. When someone went back to standardize the data they overwrote the old answers and made half of them incorrect. Never ever mess with the original data. Always do those sorts of things elsewhere so you can fix your errors when you discover them.)

Anyway. This issue with creative answers is why if you're building any sort of tracking or input form you should try to limit the allowed values to the extent possible.

Things like State and Country are obvious examples. But in the financial services industry you might also limit financial objective or income or net worth to pre-defined values or numeric ranges.

Or, if you want exact numbers, at least limit the input field so that only numbers can be provided. If you don't, you'll end with someone somewhere who puts something like, "Refuse to Disclose" in a net worth field.

So ask yourself, with the data you're dealing with, what can you standardize? Once you know that, if you're using Excel to track this kind of information, you can impose limits on those cells. You do this with Data Validation which can be found on the Data tab under Data Tools. Clicking on that option brings up the Data Validation dialogue box which gives you a variety of validation choices.

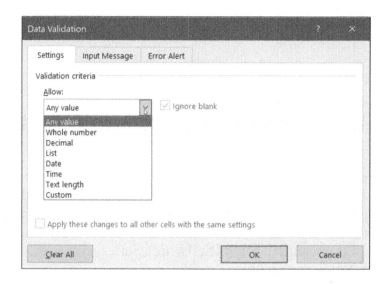

 The default is Any Value which lets you enter anything you want into that cell or range of cells.

The Whole Number option limits inputs to whole numbers (so no decimals) within a range of values you specify.

Decimal lets you input a decimal value such as 12.50.

List only allows users to input values that are on a referenced list. This is the one you would use for State, for example, and then elsewhere within the workbook you'd likely have that list on a hidden and locked worksheet. When you have a list in place it also works as a dropdown menu of options to choose from.

Date only allows the user to input a date within a specified range.

Time works the same for time.

Text length allows a user to input any text they want but limits the number of characters allowed. This is where you'd have a text box that allows up to 250 characters of explanation or comment, for example. It could also be used if you have a value that people are supposed to enter that is an exact length.

Custom lets you create custom input criteria. For example, phone number with a set format.

To apply Data Validation to a range of cells, select those cells and then click on Data Validation and then Data Validation again. Choose your validation criteria from the dropdown menu and then enter your additional parameters based upon your choice. Excel does require that you enter parameters.

If you don't care what the range is, you can enter something like a minimum of -1,000,000 and a maximum of 1,000,000 for Whole Number, for example.

But it's a good idea to consider the information you're going to collect and try to use reasonable constraints around what you know about your data. So for Income I might limit the values allowed to a minimum of zero and a maximum of 10 million under the assumption that people don't generally have a negative income and my particular firm isn't dealing with high net worth individuals.

(This is another example though of how a list can be a better choice sometimes. Because with income if I used a list of value ranges my last value in that list could be $10 million + and then I'd cover all possible answers.)

Keep Ignore Blank checked unless you are requiring that the cell have a value in them. It won't give you problems until you input a value in the cell, but once you do if Ignore Blank is unchecked you won't be able to leave that cell without there being a value in it that fits the parameters.

The Input Message Tab lets you tell the user what you want in that cell or give them other directions or information. By default the message will appear when a user clicks onto a cell with data validation if this is in place.

The message will appear with the Title portion in bold and the rest of the text unbolded. Like so:

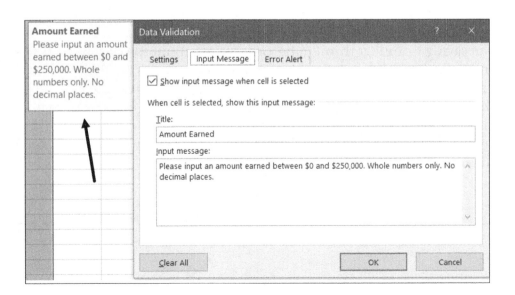

The Error Alert tab lets you generate an error alert when a user inputs the wrong value. You can choose the type of symbol to display (an ex, an exclamation mark, or a small i for information) and then you can enter a title for your error message and accompanying text.

I usually do something like "Invalid Value. Please enter a value that is a whole number between $0 and $250,000."

Click OK once you've made all of your choices.

To remove data validation, highlight the same set of cells, pull up the Data Validation dialogue box once more, and choose Clear All in the bottom left corner. If you're not sure what range of cells have Data Validation, select more than you think do and when you try to open Data Validation you'll see an error dialogue box telling you that you've selected a range with more than one type of validation and would you like to erase the current setting and continue. Clicking OK will clear the data validation from all of those cells.

(Obviously, don't do that with a range where you still wanted to keep the validation in some of the cells.)

One caution about using data validation. Be sure before you limit the inputs into a cell that you've thought through all the possible options. There is nothing more annoying than trying to input valid information and getting an error message and having no way to work around it.

I worked on a large project where we were trying to come up with these sorts of lists and when you really dig in, it isn't always as straight-forward as it seems. There are standardized lists out there for country, U.S. state, and currency code, for example, but sometimes the decision of which one to use is political. For example, do you list Burma or Myanmar? Where do you list Puerto Rico? How about including currencies that no longer exist?

All I'm saying is think it through before you roll it out to your users, test it with them once you do, and then be open to making changes as needed. Unless there's a good reason not to, I like to include an Other option with a free-text field when I'm rolling out a new list. I then monitor to see what gets entered in that field so I can either update the list with an entry I missed, provide education to those misusing the Other field, or accept that there are sometimes one-off situations that will require that Other option to always exist.

Hide or Unhide a Worksheet

To hide an entire worksheet so that other users don't see it when they open the workbook (for example, if you have dropdown lists and you want to use one worksheet for storing them), right-click on the worksheet name and select Hide.

To unhide a hidden worksheet, right-click on the name of any worksheet that's visible, choose Unhide, and then select which of the hidden worksheets you want to unhide from the Unhide dialogue box.

If you combine hiding a worksheet with protecting the workbook, no one will be able to access that hidden worksheet unless they have the password and can unprotect the workbook first.

Lock Cells or Worksheets

Since we just talked about setting up a worksheet for others to use, we should also cover how to lock a range of cells so that users are only editing the portions of the worksheet they're meant to.

For example, I had a worksheet I created once for work where users input values into the first five or six columns and then those values were used in formulas that made up the rest of the worksheet. Because I didn't want anyone to change the formulas, I locked the cells that contained those formulas.

Depending on how you go about it, you can either just lock a cell for editing or you can completely lock the cell so that a user can't even see what's in it.

Again, think about your users and their needs when doing this because it is easy to mess these things up and lock the wrong thing, not lock something that needed locked, or hide information that users actually need to see.

As another example, my company used to have us use some locked worksheets and I seem to recall one where I couldn't see the formula which meant I couldn't figure out how they needed me to enter the value they were asking for. I had to go through trial and error to figure it out. I was not happy with them by the end of that.

Anyway.

To lock a range of cells, first select the cells you want to lock, right-click, and choose Format Cells. In the Format Cells dialogue box, go to the Protection tab and click the Locked box. Then click on OK. In my worksheet the cells were already listed as protected by default, but always good to go through the process anyway. This is also means you may have to unlock cells instead to make things work correctly.

(If you also don't want users to be able to see the formulas used within those locked cells, also click the checkbox for Hidden.)

The cells are not locked at this point. You now need to add protection to the worksheet. To do that, go to the Cells section of the Home tab and click on Format. You should see an option to Protect Sheet. Select it and you'll see the Protect Sheet dialogue box.

You can input a password to lock the worksheet. Be sure you remember it if you do. If you don't input a password then anyone will be able to unprotect the sheet just by going back to the Cells section of the Home tab and choosing Unprotect Sheet from the Format dropdown.

In the Protect Sheet dialogue box there are a number of options for what you can allow users to do even when a worksheet is protected. It's a little backwards since you're choosing what you're willing to allow instead of what you're not willing to allow, but it is what it is.

The default is to allow people to select cells in the worksheet. Unless they shouldn't be copying the information for any reason, this is fine to keep.

I can also see an argument for allowing people to format columns in case they enter a value that's too big for the current column width, which I've had happen with locked worksheets in the past. (It's very annoying to enter a number, see ### instead, and not be able to widen the column.)

What to allow from the rest of that list is a judgment call. I try to lock down as much as I can without interfering with functionality, so I'd probably lock too much and then wait for complaints and fix it then. It very much depends on the environment you work in. Is it better to allow users to do most everything and then find out that they do crazy things like delete the most important column in the worksheet? Or is it better to lock it down too tight and have to fix it when someone complains, which may damage your department's reputation and could, if you have the wrong kind of boss, lead to your boss yelling at you?

That's why beta testing is so important. Make your best choice and then give it to a bunch of users to test for you before you give it to everyone. See what they complain about and adjust from there. (That's the ideal scenario.)

Once you've protected a sheet, you'll see that the options that you didn't allow are no longer available in the menus and dropdowns for that range of cells.

To remove protection from a worksheet just go back to the Format dropdown, select Unprotect Sheet, and provide your password.

You can also add or remove protection on a worksheet or for an entire Excel file (workbook) on the Review tab in the Protect section using Protect Sheet or Protect Workbook.

A Few Tips and Tricks

We're about to wrap up here but there are just a few little thoughts I had as I was going through this that I haven't covered yet but wanted to point out.

Auto Fill Options

In *Excel 2019 Beginner* I covered the basics of copying values in a cell using Copy. But I want to explore another copy option here that I use often.

Every month I transfer the sales reports I receive from each of my sales channels into an Access database. Some of those reports list the date of a transaction. Some list a date range. But what I want is a column with the current month and a column with the current year, so I always add those two columns to my Excel file before I import my data to Access.

One option for doing this is to type in the month and the year I'm working with in the first row of my data and then select those entries, use Ctrl + C, highlight the rest of the entries for those two columns in my data set, and use Ctrl + V to paste the values and then hit enter or Esc. Done.

But sometimes I'm dealing with hundreds or thousands of rows of data and Shift + Ctrl + arrow keys don't properly select the range of cells where I want to copy those values and manually selecting them with the mouse is annoying.

That's where the double-click in the corner trick comes in handy. This is where you double-click in the bottom right corner of the selected cells and Excel copies the results down the rest of the rows for you.

Your cursor should look like a little black plus sign when you're in the right place to do this.

When you use AutoFill like this, Excel will try to find a pattern in your data and will copy down that pattern. So my initial entry for October 2020 turns into November 2021 on the next row and then December 2022 and so on. It's finding a pattern for my month and my year values, which is not what I want.

Fortunately, at the bottom of the entries where it copied down there is an Auto Fill Options box that appears.

It's tiny and because of how Excel works I can't get a good picture of it, but there's a shaded cell in the top corner with unshaded cells to the side and below and a little plus sign on the right side.

Click on it and you will see a dropdown menu like the one pictured above.

As you can see, the default choice is Fill Series, but click on the button for Copy Cells and all of the values you copied down will now be identical to the first entry.

Fill Months will keep the year column untouched but change the month column. Fill Formatting Only will copy your formatting but nothing else.

Keep in mind that the AutoFill option only fills down as far as your existing data, so this only works when there are existing values in the next column over so that Excel knows how far to go.

Cell Error Messages

There are times when Excel will flag a value in a cell with an error message.

One of the times this happens is when working with formulas and when the formula in one cell is not like the formula in other nearby cells or when it doesn't do what Excel expects like uses values that are not next to the cell and skips the ones that are.

But another type of error message I wanted to talk about here is the error message you may see related to the format of the values in a cell. The most common one of these is "Number Stored as Text".

You will know there's an issue that Excel has flagged when you look at your data and see a green mark in the top left corner of a cell. Usually if it's the number stored as text error you will see this little mark for every single cell in that column. Below is an example of this from one of my vendor reports.

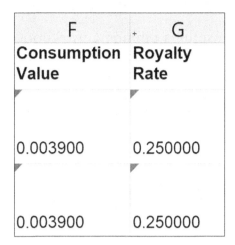

Both of these columns have values that have been flagged by Excel. You can see the four little marks in the corners above the values for both Columns F and G.

To figure out what issue Excel has, click on one of the Cells and you'll see a little alert icon appear on the top left side outside of the cell. Click on that and a dropdown menu will appear.

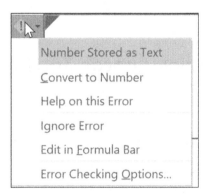

The first row in that dropdown menu tells you what the issue is. In this case Number Stored as Text. If you don't care about that, you can click on Ignore Error and the green mark will go away. If you want Excel to convert the value to a number, click on Convert to Number.

To convert all of your cells at once, highlight them all first, then click on the alert icon, and then make your choice about to handle it.

Pinned Workbooks

Another trick I've found useful is pinning a workbook (file) that I use often so that it's always right there and available when I need to open it.

To pin a file you need to have recently opened it so that it's listed in your Recent files section. Once that's true, open Excel or go to the File tab for an open file, find the file you want to pin in the Recent list, and then click on the little thumbtack pin image at the end of its name.

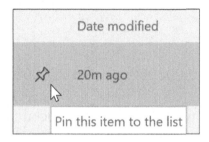

Once you do this, that file will always be available under the Pinned section so that you can easily find it no matter how many files you've opened since it was last used.

To unpin a file, just click on the pin image again.

Quick Access Toolbar

By default the Quick Access Toolbar at the top left of the screen for Excel 2019 includes the icons for save, undo, and redo. But you can add to this list if there are other tasks you complete in Excel on a regular basis that you want to have always available to you.

Just click on that little arrow at the end of the options and then click on the options you want available on the toolbar. More Commands at the bottom of the list will open the Excel Options dialogue box which contains the full list of options you can place there.

The Quick Access Toolbar is available for any Excel file you have open.

Spellcheck

This is less likely to be needed in Excel instead of Word, but can still be useful especially if you're working with a lot of text.

To check the spelling in your document click on the Spelling option in the Proofing section of the Review tab.

It's going to default to just checking from the cell(s) you have highlighted forward but will then ask if you want to also start checking from the beginning of the worksheet. Usually you'll want to say yes to that.

If it finds a spelling error the Spelling dialogue box will appear and will show you the text that Excel believes is misspelled as well as suggestions for fixing it.

Your choices are to ignore the error once, ignore it always, add that word to Excel's spelling dictionary so it doesn't flag it again, change the word once to the highlighted selection, or change the word everywhere it occurs to the highlighted selection.

Excel Options

I'm not going to go into this one in detail, but under the File tab there is an Options choice at the very bottom. Clicking on that will bring up the Excel Options dialogue box.

This is where you can go to control things like AutoCorrect.

I, for example, usually turn off the AutoCorrect option that turns a (c) into a copyright sign because of my regulatory background where I'm much more likely to be citing a rule violation involving subsection c than I am to be writing the copyright symbol. (That's under Proofing.)

You can also change your AutoRecovery settings under the Save section.

Basically, if there's something Excel does all the time that annoys you, this is most likely the place to fix it. Just be careful doing so because other users who use your version of Excel may expect it to work differently and/or you will expect new versions or other user's versions of Excel to do things for you that they don't do by default.

Zoom

If you want to increase the size of the cells you see in Excel so that the text is easier to read, you can Zoom In. If you want to decrease the size of the cells so that more are visible on the page, you can Zoom Out.

The easiest way to do this for me is in the bottom right corner. You'll see a little slider with a minus on one end, a plus on the other, a darker vertical bar somewhere in between those and a percentage shown off to the right-hand side. You can click anywhere in the space between the minus sign and the plus sign and that will increase or decrease the level of zoom in your worksheet. Left of the vertical bar to zoom out, right of the vertical bar to zoom in.

One thing that is weird about Excel is that only the cells will adjust. So dialogue boxes, dropdown menus, tab options, etc. all stay the same size and the only way to see those as bigger than they are is to zoom your monitor display through Windows (or equivalent) which can make things blurry if you zoom too far.

Another place to go for the Zoom option is the Zoom section of the View tab. You can click on the 100% option to Zoom back to 100% or click on the magnifying glass to bring up the Zoom dialogue box which has preset choices as well as a custom zoom option. Zoom to Selection will zoom in or out to fit the selected cells. If it's just one cell selected it zooms in to a space that's about four cells wide.

Help Options

Alright. What's left is basically formulas and functions which are covered in detail in the next book, more advanced topics like macros and forecasts and data models, which we're not going to cover, and a few one offs like comments that most users are not going to need so we're not going to cover either.

What I've tried to do between this guide and *Excel 2019 Beginner* is cover 98% of what the average reader will need in Excel. And, hopefully, give you a strong enough understanding of Excel that you can find the rest of what you need yourself.

If I did my job right there were times when you read this book where you were like, "Yeah, yeah, go here, do this, just like the last ten times. Got it." Because Excel is arranged in a fairly logical manner. Once you learn the logic it follows it's pretty easy to guess where things will be or how they'll work or if they can be done.

For example, I didn't cover every chart type in Excel, but after walking through the handful we did cover I'm pretty confident you could use one of the other types if you needed it.

But what if you didn't see something in Excel and don't know what it is?

That's where the help functions come in. And they're very good for the most part. A book like this helps because it provides a path to follow, but there's nothing I talk about in any of these books that you couldn't find on your own using Microsoft's help options.

So let's talk about them.

First, most of the options on the Excel toolbar have a description of what they do. All you have to do is hold your cursor over the option and it usually provides a one or two sentence summary as well as a name for the option. It will often also tell you if there's a Ctrl shortcut.

For example, Cut on the Home tab in the Clipboard section says "Cut (Ctrl + X)" and then has a description "Remove the selection and put it on the clipboard so you can paste it somewhere else."

At that point you have a basic understanding of what that particular image lets you do and you know what it's called.

If that isn't enough, some of the more complex options in Excel also have "Tell me more" at the bottom of that description which you can click on to bring up a Help task pane specific to that task. Format Painter on the Home tab is a good example.

That's the best way to pull up help for a specific topic. But to do that you have to already know where the task is.

Your other option within Excel is to click on the Help tab. (Used to be a question mark off in the corner in prior versions of Excel and now it's a tab.) From there click on Help again. That will bring up the Help task pane as well but this time it's the generic start screen.

From that point you can search for your topic or click on the various options such as Get Started, Collaborate, Formulas & Functions, etc.

F1 will also open that generic Help task pane for you.

In Excel 2019 there is now also a Show Training option under the Help tab which gives you access to Excel's help videos and text which used to be mostly hosted on the website.

Some of these are very good and often there is a visual demonstration to walk you through what you need to learn.

If your question is more along the lines of "is this possible" as opposed to "how does this specific thing work exactly.", you can also do an internet search to see if anyone has covered how to do what you want to do before. Usually they have.

So, for example, I had a user ask if it was possible to build a cell that had a slanted line in it and allowed you to input values on either side of that line. Turns out there were a number of blogs that had written ideas on how to do that.

The Community link in the Help tab will also take you to the Microsoft forums where you can ask your question or others have asked theirs.

I tend to advise against asking your own question in tech forums because they tend to attract a certain type of personality more interested in telling people they didn't ask a question properly than in giving an answer. But that's me.

Also, you can always email me (mlhumphreywriter@gmail.com). If I know or can find the answer quickly, I will definitely help out or point you in the right direction. Knowing what wasn't clear enough or wasn't covered but was needed helps me improve the books for the next edition.

And if it turns out you need really detailed help, like someone to do the work of building your worksheet for you, I do have a consulting rate. Although I'm not sure anyone outside of a large corporate environment would want to pay it.

Conclusion

Alright. That's it. That's intermediate Excel. If you want to learn more about formulas and functions, then the next book in the series *Excel 2019 Formulas and Functions* will definitely do that for you. If you want to move on to macros or SQL, I'm afraid you'll have to find someone else to cover those topics.

But I do hope at this point that you feel pretty confident that you can use Excel for day-to-day purposes and to do some more complex data analysis.

Don't be scared to experiment. Half of what I've learned in Excel was because I decided it should be possible to do something and went looking for how to do it.

You can almost always undo it if it goes wrong. Ctrl + Z is your friend.

Also, save a safe version of your file if you're experimenting or building a worksheet with a lot of moving parts.

I do this all the time when initially building a worksheet. I'll figure out Column A's calculation and save a draft of the file. Then I'll take a copy of the file and work on Column B's calculation. And so on and so on until the whole thing is built. That lets me not lose everything if on Column E's calculation I suddenly realize I messed something up that can't be fixed.

By using the YYYYMMDD date format in the file name and version numbers if needed you can easily sort your files by name and find the most recent version. (So 20201101 Sales Revenue Calculation, 20201102 Sales Revenue Calculation v1, 20201102 Sales Revenue Calculation v2, etc.)

Take risks. Try new things. Don't beat yourself up if you get it wrong the first time. This is a learning process and I've sometimes learned the best lessons from my failures.

Alright, then. Best of luck. Reach out if you get stuck.

INDEX

About the Author

M.L. Humphrey is a former stockbroker with a degree in Economics from Stanford and an MBA from Wharton who has spent close to twenty years as a regulator and consultant in the financial services industry.

You can reach M.L. Humphrey at:

mlhumphreywriter@gmail.com

or at

www.mlhumphrey.com

Made in the USA
Middletown, DE
19 February 2021